**HBR'S
10
MUST
READS**

On
Career
Resilience

HBR's 10 Must Reads series is the definitive collection of ideas and best practices for aspiring and experienced leaders alike. These books offer essential reading selected from the pages of *Harvard Business Review* on topics critical to the success of every manager.

Titles include:

HBR'S 10 MUST READS

On
Career
Resilience

HARVARD BUSINESS REVIEW PRESS
Boston, Massachusetts

Copyright 2021 Harvard Business School Publishing Corporation
All rights reserved
Printed and bound in India by Replika Press Pvt. Ltd.
10 9 8 7 6 5 4 3 2

The web addresses referenced in this book were live and correct at the time of the book's publication but may be subject to change.

Library of Congress Cataloging-in-Publication Data is forthcoming.

ISBN: 978-1-64782-059-6
eISBN: 978-1-64782-060-2

Contents

HBR'S 10 MUST READS

On
Career
Resilience

Managing Oneself

by Peter F. Drucker

HISTORY'S GREAT ACHIEVERS—a Napoléon, a da Vinci, a Mozart—have always managed themselves. That, in large measure, is what makes them great achievers. But they are rare exceptions, so unusual both in their talents and their accomplishments as to be considered outside the boundaries of ordinary human existence. Now, most of us, even those of us with modest endowments, will have to learn to manage ourselves. We will have to learn to develop ourselves. We will have to place ourselves where we can make the greatest contribution. And we will have to stay mentally alert and engaged during a 50-year working life, which means knowing how and when to change the work we do.

What Are My Strengths?

Most people think they know what they are good at. They are usually wrong. More often, people know what they are not good at—and even then more people are wrong than right. And yet, a person can perform only from strength. One cannot build performance on weaknesses, let alone on something one cannot do at all.

Throughout history, people had little need to know their strengths. A person was born into a position and a line of work: The peasant's son would also be a peasant; the artisan's daughter, an artisan's wife; and so on. But now people have choices. We need to know our strengths in order to know where we belong.

The only way to discover your strengths is through feedback analysis. Whenever you make a key decision or take a key action, write down what you expect will happen. Nine or 12 months later, compare the actual results with your expectations. I have been practicing this method for 15 to 20 years now, and every time I do it, I am surprised. The feedback analysis showed me, for instance—and to my great surprise—that I have an intuitive understanding of technical people, whether they are engineers or accountants or market researchers. It also showed me that I don't really resonate with generalists.

Feedback analysis is by no means new. It was invented sometime in the fourteenth century by an otherwise totally obscure German theologian and picked up quite independently, some 150 years later, by John Calvin and Ignatius of Loyola, each of whom incorporated it into the practice of his followers. In fact, the steadfast focus on performance and results that this habit produces explains why the institutions these two men founded, the Calvinist church and the Jesuit order, came to dominate Europe within 30 years.

Practiced consistently, this simple method will show you within a fairly short period of time, maybe two or three years, where your strengths lie—and this is the most important thing to know. The method will show you what you are doing or failing to do that deprives you of the full benefits of your strengths. It will show you where you are not particularly competent. And finally, it will show you where you have no strengths and cannot perform.

Several implications for action follow from feedback analysis. First and foremost, concentrate on your strengths. Put yourself where your strengths can produce results.

Second, work on improving your strengths. Analysis will rapidly show where you need to improve skills or acquire new ones. It will also show the gaps in your knowledge—and those can usually be filled. Mathematicians are born, but everyone can learn trigonometry.

Third, discover where your intellectual arrogance is causing disabling ignorance and overcome it. Far too many people—especially

Idea in Brief

We live in an age of unprecedented opportunity: If you've got ambition, drive, and smarts, you can rise to the top of your chosen profession—regardless of where you started out. But with opportunity comes responsibility. Companies today aren't managing their knowledge workers' careers. Rather, we must each be our own chief executive officer.

Simply put, it's up to you to carve out your place in the work world and know when to change course. And it's up to you to keep yourself engaged and productive during a work life that may span some 50 years.

To do all of these things well, you'll need to cultivate a deep understanding of yourself. What are your most valuable strengths and most dangerous weaknesses? Equally important, how do you learn and work with others? What are your most deeply held values? And in what type of work environment can you make the greatest contribution?

The implication is clear: Only when you operate from a combination of your strengths and self-knowledge can you achieve true—and lasting—excellence.

people with great expertise in one area—are contemptuous of knowledge in other areas or believe that being bright is a substitute for knowledge. First-rate engineers, for instance, tend to take pride in not knowing anything about people. Human beings, they believe, are much too disorderly for the good engineering mind. Human resources professionals, by contrast, often pride themselves on their ignorance of elementary accounting or of quantitative methods altogether. But taking pride in such ignorance is self-defeating. Go to work on acquiring the skills and knowledge you need to fully realize your strengths.

It is equally essential to remedy your bad habits—the things you do or fail to do that inhibit your effectiveness and performance. Such habits will quickly show up in the feedback. For example, a planner may find that his beautiful plans fail because he does not follow through on them. Like so many brilliant people, he believes that ideas move mountains. But bulldozers move mountains; ideas show where the bulldozers should go to work. This planner will have to learn that the work does not stop when the plan is completed. He

3

Idea in Practice

To build a life of excellence, begin by asking yourself these questions:

"What are my strengths?"

To accurately identify your strengths, use **feedback analysis**. Every time you make a key decision, write down the outcome you expect. Several months later, compare the actual results with your expected results. Look for patterns in what you're seeing: What results are you skilled at generating? What abilities do you need to enhance in order to get the results you want? What unproductive habits are preventing you from creating the outcomes you desire? In identifying opportunities for improvement, don't waste time cultivating skill areas where you have little competence. Instead, concentrate on—and build on—your strengths.

"How do I work?"

In what ways do you work best? Do you process information most effectively by reading it, or by hearing others discuss it? Do you accomplish the most by working with other people, or by working alone? Do you perform best while making decisions, or while advising others on key matters? Are you in top form when things get stressful, or do you function optimally in a highly predictable environment?

"What are my values?"

What are your ethics? What do you see as your most important responsibilities for living a worthy, ethical life? Do your organization's ethics resonate with your own values? If not, your career will likely be marked by frustration and poor performance.

"Where do I belong?"

Consider your strengths, preferred work style, and values. Based on these qualities, in what kind of work environment would you fit in best? Find the perfect fit, and you'll transform yourself from a merely acceptable employee into a star performer.

"What can I contribute?"

In earlier eras, companies told businesspeople what their contribution should be. Today, you have choices. To decide how you can best enhance your organization's performance, first ask what the situation requires. Based on your strengths, work style, and values, how might you make the greatest contribution to your organization's efforts?

must find people to carry out the plan and explain it to them. He must adapt and change it as he puts it into action. And finally, he must decide when to stop pushing the plan.

At the same time, feedback will also reveal when the problem is a lack of manners. Manners are the lubricating oil of an organization. It is a law of nature that two moving bodies in contact with each other create friction. This is as true for human beings as it is for inanimate objects. Manners—simple things like saying "please" and "thank you" and knowing a person's name or asking after her family—enable two people to work together whether they like each other or not. Bright people, especially bright young people, often do not understand this. If analysis shows that someone's brilliant work fails again and again as soon as cooperation from others is required, it probably indicates a lack of courtesy—that is, a lack of manners.

Comparing your expectations with your results also indicates what not to do. We all have a vast number of areas in which we have no talent or skill and little chance of becoming even mediocre. In those areas a person—and especially a knowledge worker—should not take on work, jobs, and assignments. One should waste as little effort as possible on improving areas of low competence. It takes far more energy and work to improve from incompetence to mediocrity than it takes to improve from first-rate performance to excellence. And yet most people—especially most teachers and most organizations—concentrate on making incompetent performers into mediocre ones. Energy, resources, and time should go instead to making a competent person into a star performer.

How Do I Perform?

Amazingly few people know how they get things done. Indeed, most of us do not even know that different people work and perform differently. Too many people work in ways that are not their ways, and that almost guarantees nonperformance. For knowledge workers, How do I perform? may be an even more important question than What are my strengths?

Like one's strengths, how one performs is unique. It is a matter of personality. Whether personality be a matter of nature or nurture, it surely is formed long before a person goes to work. And *how* a person performs is a given, just as *what* a person is good at or not good at is a given. A person's way of performing can be slightly modified, but it is unlikely to be completely changed—and certainly not easily. Just as people achieve results by doing what they are good at, they also achieve results by working in ways that they best perform. A few common personality traits usually determine how a person performs.

Am I a reader or a listener?

The first thing to know is whether you are a reader or a listener. Far too few people even know that there are readers and listeners and that people are rarely both. Even fewer know which of the two they themselves are. But some examples will show how damaging such ignorance can be.

When Dwight Eisenhower was Supreme Commander of the Allied forces in Europe, he was the darling of the press. His press conferences were famous for their style—General Eisenhower showed total command of whatever question he was asked, and he was able to describe a situation and explain a policy in two or three beautifully polished and elegant sentences. Ten years later, the same journalists who had been his admirers held President Eisenhower in open contempt. He never addressed the questions, they complained, but rambled on endlessly about something else. And they constantly ridiculed him for butchering the King's English in incoherent and ungrammatical answers.

Eisenhower apparently did not know that he was a reader, not a listener. When he was Supreme Commander in Europe, his aides made sure that every question from the press was presented in writing at least half an hour before a conference was to begin. And then Eisenhower was in total command. When he became president, he succeeded two listeners, Franklin D. Roosevelt and Harry Truman. Both men knew themselves to be listeners and both enjoyed free-for-all press conferences. Eisenhower may have felt that he had to do what his two predecessors had done. As a result, he never even heard the questions journalists asked. And Eisenhower is not even an extreme case of a nonlistener.

A few years later, Lyndon Johnson destroyed his presidency, in large measure, by not knowing that he was a listener. His predecessor, John Kennedy, was a reader who had assembled a brilliant group of writers as his assistants, making sure that they wrote to him before discussing their memos in person. Johnson kept these people on his staff—and they kept on writing. He never, apparently, understood one word of what they wrote. Yet as a senator, Johnson had been superb; for parliamentarians have to be, above all, listeners.

Few listeners can be made, or can make themselves, into competent readers—and vice versa. The listener who tries to be a reader will, therefore, suffer the fate of Lyndon Johnson, whereas the reader who tries to be a listener will suffer the fate of Dwight Eisenhower. They will not perform or achieve.

How do I learn?

The second thing to know about how one performs is to know how one learns. Many first-class writers—Winston Churchill is but one example—do poorly in school. They tend to remember their schooling as pure torture. Yet few of their classmates remember it the same way. They may not have enjoyed the school very much, but the worst they suffered was boredom. The explanation is that writers do not, as a rule, learn by listening and reading. They learn by writing. Because schools do not allow them to learn this way, they get poor grades.

Schools everywhere are organized on the assumption that there is only one right way to learn and that it is the same way for everybody. But to be forced to learn the way a school teaches is sheer hell for students who learn differently. Indeed, there are probably half a dozen different ways to learn.

There are people, like Churchill, who learn by writing. Some people learn by taking copious notes. Beethoven, for example, left behind an enormous number of sketchbooks, yet he said he never actually looked at them when he composed. Asked why he kept them, he is reported to have replied, "If I don't write it down immediately, I forget it right away. If I put it into a sketchbook, I never forget it and I never have to look it up again." Some people learn by doing. Others learn by hearing themselves talk.

A chief executive I know who converted a small and mediocre family business into the leading company in its industry was one of those people who learn by talking. He was in the habit of calling his entire senior staff into his office once a week and then talking at them for two or three hours. He would raise policy issues and argue three different positions on each one. He rarely asked his associates for comments or questions; he simply needed an audience to hear himself talk. That's how he learned. And although he is a fairly extreme case, learning through talking is by no means an unusual method. Successful trial lawyers learn the same way, as do many medical diagnosticians (and so do I).

Of all the important pieces of self-knowledge, understanding how you learn is the easiest to acquire. When I ask people, "How do you learn?" most of them know the answer. But when I ask, "Do you act on this knowledge?" few answer yes. And yet, acting on this knowledge is the key to performance; or rather, *not* acting on this knowledge condemns one to nonperformance.

Am I a reader or a listener? and How do I learn? are the first questions to ask. But they are by no means the only ones. To manage yourself effectively, you also have to ask, Do I work well with people, or am I a loner? And if you do work well with people, you then must ask, In what relationship?

Some people work best as subordinates. General George Patton, the great American military hero of World War II, is a prime example. Patton was America's top troop commander. Yet when he was proposed for an independent command, General George Marshall, the U.S. chief of staff—and probably the most successful picker of men in U.S. history—said, "Patton is the best subordinate the American army has ever produced, but he would be the worst commander."

Some people work best as team members. Others work best alone. Some are exceptionally talented as coaches and mentors; others are simply incompetent as mentors.

Another crucial question is, Do I produce results as a decision maker or as an adviser? A great many people perform best as advisers but cannot take the burden and pressure of making the decision. A good many other people, by contrast, need an adviser to force themselves to think; then they can make decisions and act on them with speed, self-confidence, and courage.

This is a reason, by the way, that the number two person in an organization often fails when promoted to the number one position. The top spot requires a decision maker. Strong decision makers often put somebody they trust into the number two spot as their adviser—and in that position the person is outstanding. But in the number one spot, the same person fails. He or she knows what the decision should be but cannot accept the responsibility of actually making it.

Other important questions to ask include, Do I perform well under stress, or do I need a highly structured and predictable environment? Do I work best in a big organization or a small one? Few people work well in all kinds of environments. Again and again, I have seen people who were very successful in large organizations flounder miserably when they moved into smaller ones. And the reverse is equally true.

The conclusion bears repeating: Do not try to change yourself—you are unlikely to succeed. But work hard to improve the way you perform. And try not to take on work you cannot perform or will only perform poorly.

What Are My Values?

To be able to manage yourself, you finally have to ask, What are my values? This is not a question of ethics. With respect to ethics, the rules are the same for everybody, and the test is a simple one. I call it the "mirror test."

In the early years of this century, the most highly respected diplomat of all the great powers was the German ambassador in London. He was clearly destined for great things—to become his country's foreign minister, at least, if not its federal chancellor. Yet in 1906 he abruptly resigned rather than preside over a dinner given by the diplomatic corps for Edward VII. The king was a notorious womanizer and made it clear what kind of dinner he wanted. The ambassador is reported to have said, "I refuse to see a pimp in the mirror in the morning when I shave."

That is the mirror test. Ethics requires that you ask yourself, What kind of person do I want to see in the mirror in the morning? What is ethical behavior in one kind of organization or situation is ethical behavior in another. But ethics is only part of a value system—especially of an organization's value system.

To work in an organization whose value system is unacceptable or incompatible with one's own condemns a person both to frustration and to nonperformance.

Consider the experience of a highly successful human resources executive whose company was acquired by a bigger organization. After the acquisition, she was promoted to do the kind of work she did best, which included selecting people for important positions. The executive deeply believed that a company should hire people for such positions from the outside only after exhausting all the inside possibilities. But her new company believed in first looking outside "to bring in fresh blood." There is something to be said for both approaches—in my experience, the proper one is to do some of both. They are, however, fundamentally incompatible—not as policies but as values. They bespeak different views of the relationship between organizations and people; different views of the responsibility of an organization to its people and their development; and different views of a person's most important contribution to an enterprise. After several years of frustration, the executive quit—at considerable financial loss. Her values and the values of the organization simply were not compatible.

Similarly, whether a pharmaceutical company tries to obtain results by making constant, small improvements or by achieving occasional, highly expensive, and risky "breakthroughs" is not primarily an economic question. The results of either strategy may be pretty much the same. At bottom, there is a conflict between a value system that sees the company's contribution in terms of helping physicians do better what they already do and a value system that is oriented toward making scientific discoveries.

Whether a business should be run for short-term results or with a focus on the long term is likewise a question of values. Financial analysts believe that businesses can be run for both simultaneously. Successful businesspeople know better. To be sure, every company has to produce short-term results. But in any conflict between short-term results and long-term growth, each company will determine its own priority. This is not primarily a disagreement about economics. It is fundamentally a value conflict regarding the function of a business and the responsibility of management.

Value conflicts are not limited to business organizations. One of the fastest-growing pastoral churches in the United States measures success by the number of new parishioners. Its leadership believes that what matters is how many newcomers join the congregation. The Good Lord will then minister to their spiritual needs or at least to the needs of a sufficient percentage. Another pastoral, evangelical church believes that what matters is people's spiritual growth. The church eases out newcomers who join but do not enter into its spiritual life.

Again, this is not a matter of numbers. At first glance, it appears that the second church grows more slowly. But it retains a far larger proportion of newcomers than the first one does. Its growth, in other words, is more solid. This is also not a theological problem, or only secondarily so. It is a problem about values. In a public debate, one pastor argued, "Unless you first come to church, you will never find the gate to the Kingdom of Heaven."

"No," answered the other. "Until you first look for the gate to the Kingdom of Heaven, you don't belong in church."

Organizations, like people, have values. To be effective in an organization, a person's values must be compatible with the organization's values. They do not need to be the same, but they must be close enough to coexist. Otherwise, the person will not only be frustrated but also will not produce results.

A person's strengths and the way that person performs rarely conflict; the two are complementary. But there is sometimes a conflict between a person's values and his or her strengths. What one does well—even very well and successfully—may not fit with one's value system. In that case, the work may not appear to be worth devoting one's life to (or even a substantial portion thereof).

If I may, allow me to interject a personal note. Many years ago, I too had to decide between my values and what I was doing successfully. I was doing very well as a young investment banker in London in the mid-1930s, and the work clearly fit my strengths. Yet I did not see myself making a contribution as an asset manager. People, I realized, were what I valued, and I saw no point in being the richest man in the cemetery. I had no money and no other job prospects. Despite the continuing Depression, I quit—and it was the right thing to do. Values, in other words, are and should be the ultimate test.

Where Do I Belong?

A small number of people know very early where they belong. Mathematicians, musicians, and cooks, for instance, are usually mathematicians, musicians, and cooks by the time they are four or five years old. Physicians usually decide on their careers in their teens, if not earlier. But most people, especially highly gifted people, do not really know where they belong until they are well past their mid-twenties. By that time, however, they should know the answers to the three questions: What are my strengths? How do I perform? and, What are my values? And then they can and should decide where they belong.

Or rather, they should be able to decide where they do *not* belong. The person who has learned that he or she does not perform well in a big organization should have learned to say no to a position in one. The person who has learned that he or she is not a decision maker should have learned to say no to a decision-making assignment. A General Patton (who probably never learned this himself) should have learned to say no to an independent command.

Equally important, knowing the answer to these questions enables a person to say to an opportunity, an offer, or an assignment, "Yes, I will do that. But this is the way I should be doing it. This is the way it should be structured. This is the way the relationships should be. These are the kind of results you should expect from me, and in this time frame, because this is who I am."

Successful careers are not planned. They develop when people are prepared for opportunities because they know their strengths, their method of work, and their values. Knowing where one belongs can transform an ordinary person—hardworking and competent but otherwise mediocre—into an outstanding performer.

What Should I Contribute?

Throughout history, the great majority of people never had to ask the question, What should I contribute? They were told what to contribute, and their tasks were dictated either by the work itself—as it was for the peasant or artisan—or by a master or a mistress—as it was for domestic servants. And until very recently, it was taken for granted that most people were subordinates who did as they were told. Even in the 1950s and 1960s, the new knowledge workers (the so-called organization men) looked to their company's personnel department to plan their careers.

Then in the late 1960s, no one wanted to be told what to do any longer. Young men and women began to ask, What do *I* want to do? And what they heard was that the way to contribute was to "do your own thing." But this solution was as wrong as the organization men's had been. Very few of the people who believed that doing one's own thing would lead to contribution, self-fulfillment, and success achieved any of the three.

But still, there is no return to the old answer of doing what you are told or assigned to do. Knowledge workers in particular have to learn to ask a question that has not been asked before: What *should* my contribution be? To answer it, they must address three distinct elements: What does the situation require? Given my strengths, my way of performing, and my values, how can I make the greatest contribution to what needs to be done? And finally, What results have to be achieved to make a difference?

Consider the experience of a newly appointed hospital administrator. The hospital was big and prestigious, but it had been coasting on its reputation for 30 years. The new administrator decided that his contribution should be to establish a standard of excellence in one important area within two years. He chose to focus on the emergency room, which was big, visible, and sloppy. He decided that every patient who came into the ER had to be seen by a qualified nurse within 60 seconds. Within 12 months, the hospital's emergency room had become a model for all hospitals in the United States, and within another two years, the whole hospital had been transformed.

As this example suggests, it is rarely possible—or even particularly fruitful—to look too far ahead. A plan can usually cover no more than 18 months and still be reasonably clear and specific. So the question in most cases should be, Where and how can I achieve results that will make a difference within the next year and a half? The answer must balance several things. First, the results should be hard to achieve—they should require "stretching," to use the current buzzword. But also, they should be within reach. To aim at results that cannot be achieved—or that can be only under the most unlikely circumstances—is not being ambitious; it is being foolish. Second, the results should be meaningful. They should make a difference. Finally, results should be visible and, if at all possible, measurable. From this will come a course of action: what to do, where and how to start, and what goals and deadlines to set.

Responsibility for Relationships

Very few people work by themselves and achieve results by themselves—a few great artists, a few great scientists, a few great athletes. Most people work with others and are effective with other people. That is true whether they are members of an organization or independently employed. Managing yourself requires taking responsibility for relationships. This has two parts.

The first is to accept the fact that other people are as much individuals as you yourself are. They perversely insist on behaving like human beings. This means that they too have their strengths; they too have their ways of getting things done; they too have their values. To be effective, therefore, you have to know the strengths, the performance modes, and the values of your coworkers.

That sounds obvious, but few people pay attention to it. Typical is the person who was trained to write reports in his or her first assignment because that boss was a reader. Even if the next boss is a listener, the person goes on writing reports that, invariably, produce no results. Invariably the boss will think the employee is stupid, incompetent, and lazy, and he or she will fail. But that could have been avoided if the employee had only looked at the new boss and analyzed how *this* boss performs.

Bosses are neither a title on the organization chart nor a "function." They are individuals and are entitled to do their work in the way they do it best. It is incumbent on the people who work with them to observe them, to find out how they work, and to adapt themselves to what makes their bosses most effective. This, in fact, is the secret of "managing" the boss.

The same holds true for all your coworkers. Each works his or her way, not your way. And each is entitled to work in his or her way. What matters is whether they perform and what their values are. As for how they perform—each is likely to do it differently. The first secret of effectiveness is to understand the people you work with and depend on so that you can make use of their strengths, their ways of working, and their values. Working relationships are as much based on the people as they are on the work.

The second part of relationship responsibility is taking responsibility for communication. Whenever I, or any other consultant, start to work with an organization, the first thing I hear about are all the personality conflicts. Most of these arise from the fact that people do not know what other people are doing and how they do their work, or what contribution the other people are concentrating on and what results they expect. And the reason they do not know is that they have not asked and therefore have not been told.

This failure to ask reflects human stupidity less than it reflects human history. Until recently, it was unnecessary to tell any of these things to anybody. In the medieval city, everyone in a district plied the same trade. In the countryside, everyone in a valley planted the same crop as soon as the frost was out of the ground. Even those few people who did things that were not "common" worked alone, so they did not have to tell anyone what they were doing.

Today the great majority of people work with others who have different tasks and responsibilities. The marketing vice president may have come out of sales and know everything about sales, but she knows nothing about the things she has never done—pricing, advertising, packaging, and the like. So the people who do these things must make sure that the marketing vice president understands what they are trying to do, why they are trying to do it, how they are going to do it, and what results to expect.

If the marketing vice president does not understand what these high-grade knowledge specialists are doing, it is primarily their fault, not hers. They have not educated her. Conversely, it is the marketing vice president's responsibility to make sure that all of her coworkers understand how she looks at marketing: what her goals are, how she works, and what she expects of herself and of each one of them.

Even people who understand the importance of taking responsibility for relationships often do not communicate sufficiently with their associates. They are afraid of being thought presumptuous or inquisitive or stupid. They are wrong. Whenever someone goes to his or her associates and says, "This is what I am good at. This is how I work. These are my values. This is the contribution I plan to concentrate on and the results I should be expected to deliver," the response is always, "This is most helpful. But why didn't you tell me earlier?"

And one gets the same reaction—without exception, in my experience—if one continues by asking, "And what do I need to know about your strengths, how you perform, your values, and your proposed contribution?" In fact, knowledge workers should request this of everyone with whom they work, whether as subordinate, superior, colleague, or team member. And again, whenever this is done, the reaction is always, "Thanks for asking me. But why didn't you ask me earlier?"

Organizations are no longer built on force but on trust. The existence of trust between people does not necessarily mean that they like one another. It means that they understand one another. Taking responsibility for relationships is therefore an absolute necessity. It is a duty. Whether one is a member of the organization, a consultant to it, a supplier, or a distributor, one owes that responsibility to all one's coworkers: those whose work one depends on as well as those who depend on one's own work.

The Second Half of Your Life

When work for most people meant manual labor, there was no need to worry about the second half of your life. You simply kept on doing what you had always done. And if you were lucky enough to survive 40 years of hard work in the mill or on the railroad, you were quite happy to spend the rest of your life doing nothing. Today, however, most work is knowledge work, and knowledge workers are not "finished" after 40 years on the job, they are merely bored.

We hear a great deal of talk about the midlife crisis of the executive. It is mostly boredom. At 45, most executives have reached the peak of their business careers, and they know it. After 20 years of doing very much the same kind of work, they are very good at their jobs. But they are not learning or contributing or deriving challenge and satisfaction from the job. And yet they are still likely to face another 20 if not 25 years of work. That is why managing oneself increasingly leads one to begin a second career.

There are three ways to develop a second career. The first is actually to start one. Often this takes nothing more than moving from one kind of organization to another: the divisional controller in a large corporation, for instance, becomes the controller of a medium-sized hospital. But there are also growing numbers of people who move into different lines of work altogether: the business executive or government official who enters the ministry at 45, for instance; or the midlevel manager who leaves corporate life after 20 years to attend law school and become a small-town attorney.

We will see many more second careers undertaken by people who have achieved modest success in their first jobs. Such people have substantial skills, and they know how to work. They need a community—the house is empty with the children gone—and they need income as well. But above all, they need challenge.

The second way to prepare for the second half of your life is to develop a parallel career. Many people who are very successful in their first careers stay in the work they have been doing, either on a full-time or part-time or consulting basis. But in addition, they create a parallel job, usually in a nonprofit organization, that takes another ten hours of work a week. They might take over the administration of their church, for instance, or the presidency of the local Girl Scouts council. They might run the battered women's shelter, work as a children's librarian for the local public library, sit on the school board, and so on.

Finally, there are the social entrepreneurs. These are usually people who have been very successful in their first careers. They love their work, but it no longer challenges them. In many cases they keep on doing what they have been doing all along but spend less and less of their time on it. They also start another activity, usually a nonprofit. My friend Bob Buford, for example, built a very successful television company that he still runs. But he has also founded and built a successful nonprofit organization that works with Protestant churches, and he is building another to teach social entrepreneurs how to manage their own nonprofit ventures while still running their original businesses.

People who manage the second half of their lives may always be a minority. The majority may "retire on the job" and count the years until their actual retirement. But it is this minority, the men and women who see a long working-life expectancy as an opportunity both for themselves and for society, who will become leaders and models.

There is one prerequisite for managing the second half of your life: You must begin long before you enter it. When it first became clear 30 years ago that working-life expectancies were lengthening very fast, many observers (including myself) believed that retired people would increasingly become volunteers for nonprofit institutions. That has not happened. If one does not begin to volunteer before one is 40 or so, one will not volunteer once past 60.

Similarly, all the social entrepreneurs I know began to work in their chosen second enterprise long before they reached their peak in their original business. Consider the example of a successful lawyer, the legal counsel to a large corporation, who has started a venture to establish model schools in his state. He began to do volunteer legal work for the schools when he was around 35. He was elected to the school board at age 40. At age 50, when he had amassed a fortune, he started his own enterprise to build and to run model schools. He is, however, still working nearly full-time as the lead counsel in the company he helped found as a young lawyer.

There is another reason to develop a second major interest, and to develop it early. No one can expect to live very long without experiencing a serious setback in his or her life or work. There is the competent engineer who is passed over for promotion at age 45. There is the competent college professor who realizes at age 42 that she will never get a professorship at a big university, even though she may be fully qualified for it. There are tragedies in one's family life: the breakup of one's marriage or the loss of a child. At such times, a second major interest—not just a hobby—may make all the difference. The engineer, for example, now knows that he has not been very successful in his job. But in his outside activity—as church treasurer, for example—he is a success. One's family may break up, but in that outside activity there is still a community.

In a society in which success has become so terribly important, having options will become increasingly vital. Historically, there was no such thing as "success." The overwhelming majority of people did not expect anything but to stay in their "proper station," as an old English prayer has it. The only mobility was downward mobility.

In a knowledge society, however, we expect everyone to be a success. This is clearly an impossibility. For a great many people, there is at best an absence of failure. Wherever there is success, there has to be failure. And then it is vitally important for the individual, and equally for the individual's family, to have an area in which he or she can contribute, make a difference, and be *somebody*. That means finding a second area—whether in a second career, a parallel career, or a social venture—that offers an opportunity for being a leader, for being respected, for being a success.

The challenges of managing oneself may seem obvious, if not elementary. And the answers may seem self-evident to the point of appearing naïve. But managing oneself requires new and unprecedented things from the individual, and especially from the knowledge worker. In effect, managing oneself demands that each knowledge worker think and behave like a chief executive officer. Further, the shift from manual workers who do as they are told to knowledge workers who have to manage themselves profoundly challenges social structure. Every existing society, even the most individualistic one, takes two things for granted, if only subconsciously: that organizations outlive workers, and that most people stay put.

But today the opposite is true. Knowledge workers outlive organizations, and they are mobile. The need to manage oneself is therefore creating a revolution in human affairs.

Originally published in January 1999. Reprint R0501K

How to Play to Your Strengths

by Laura Morgan Roberts, Gretchen Spreitzer, Jane Dutton, Robert Quinn, Emily Heaphy, and Brianna Barker Caza

MOST FEEDBACK ACCENTUATES THE NEGATIVE. During formal employee evaluations, discussions invariably focus on "opportunities for improvement," even if the overall evaluation is laudatory. Informally, the sting of criticism lasts longer than the balm of praise. Multiple studies have shown that people pay keen attention to negative information. For example, when asked to recall important emotional events, people remember four negative memories for every positive one. No wonder most executives give and receive performance reviews with all the enthusiasm of a child on the way to the dentist.

Traditional, corrective feedback has its place, of course; every organization must filter out failing employees and ensure that everyone performs at an expected level of competence. Unfortunately, feedback that ferrets out flaws can lead otherwise talented managers to overinvest in shoring up or papering over their perceived weaknesses, or forcing themselves onto an ill-fitting template. Ironically, such a focus on problem areas prevents companies from reaping the best performance from its people. After all, it's a rare baseball player who is equally good at every position. Why should a natural third baseman labor to develop his skills as a right fielder?

The alternative, as the Gallup Organization researchers Marcus Buckingham, Donald Clifton, and others have suggested, is to foster excellence in the third baseman by identifying and harnessing his unique strengths. It is a paradox of human psychology that while people remember criticism, they respond to praise. The former makes them defensive and therefore unlikely to change, while the latter produces confidence and the desire to perform better. Managers who build up their strengths can reach their highest potential. This positive approach does not pretend to ignore or deny the problems that traditional feedback mechanisms identify. Rather, it offers a separate and unique feedback experience that counterbalances negative input. It allows managers to tap into strengths they may or may not be aware of and so contribute more to their organizations.

During the past few years, we have developed a powerful tool to help people understand and leverage their individual talents. Called the Reflected Best Self (RBS) exercise, our method allows managers to develop a sense of their "personal best" in order to increase their future potential. The RBS exercise is but one example of new approaches springing from an area of research called positive organizational scholarship (POS). Just as psychologists know that people respond better to praise than to criticism, organizational behavior scholars are finding that when companies focus on positive attributes such as resilience and trust, they can reap impressive bottom-line returns. (For more on this research, visit the Center for Positive Organizations.) Thousands of executives, as well as tomorrow's leaders enrolled in business schools around the world, have completed the RBS exercise.

In this article, we will walk you through the RBS exercise step-by-step and describe the insights and results it can yield. Before we proceed, however, a few caveats are in order. First, understand that the tool is not designed to stroke your ego; its purpose is to assist you in developing a plan for more effective action. (Without such a plan, you'll keep running in place.) Second, the lessons generated from the RBS exercise can elude you if you don't pay sincere attention to them. If you are too burdened by time pressures and job demands, you may just file the information away and forget about

Idea in Brief

Most feedback accentuates the negative. During formal employee evaluations, discussions invariably focus on "opportunities for improvement," even if the overall evaluation is laudatory. No wonder most executives—and their direct reports—dread them.

Traditional, corrective feedback has its place, of course; every organization must filter out failing employees and ensure that everyone performs at an expected level of competence. But too much emphasis on problem areas prevents companies from reaping the best from their people. After all, it's a rare baseball player who is equally good at every position. Why should a natural third baseman labor to develop his skills as a right fielder?

This article presents a tool to help you understand and leverage your strengths. Called the Reflected Best Self (RBS) exercise, it offers a unique feedback experience that counterbalances negative input. It allows you to tap into talents you may or may not be aware of and so increase your career potential.

To begin the RBS exercise, you first need to solicit comments from family, friends, colleagues, and teachers, asking them to give specific examples of times in which those strengths were particularly beneficial. Next, you need to search for common themes in the feedback, organizing them in a table to develop a clear picture of your strong suits. Third, you must write a self-portrait—a description of yourself that summarizes and distills the accumulated information. And finally, you need to redesign your personal job description to build on what you're good at.

The RBS exercise will help you discover who you are at the top of your game. Once you're aware of your best self, you can shape the positions you choose to play—both now and in the next phase of your career.

it. To be effective, the exercise requires commitment, diligence, and follow-through. It may even be helpful to have a coach keep you on task. Third, it's important to conduct the RBS exercise at a different time of year than the traditional performance review so that negative feedback from traditional mechanisms doesn't interfere with the results of the exercise.

Used correctly, the RBS exercise can help you tap into unrecognized and unexplored areas of potential. Armed with a constructive, systematic process for gathering and analyzing data about your best self, you can burnish your performance at work.

Step 1: Identify Respondents and Ask for Feedback

The first task in the exercise is to collect feedback from a variety of people inside and outside work. By gathering input from a variety of sources—family members, past and present colleagues, friends, teachers, and so on—you can develop a much broader and richer understanding of yourself than you can from a standard performance evaluation.

As we describe the process of the Reflected Best Self exercise, we will highlight the experience of Robert Duggan (not his real name), whose self-discovery process is typical of the managers we've observed. Having retired from a successful career in the military at a fairly young age and earned an MBA from a top business school, Robert accepted a midlevel management position at an IT services firm. Despite strong credentials and leadership experience, Robert remained stuck in the same position year after year. His performance evaluations were generally good but not strong enough to put him on the high-potential track. Disengaged, frustrated, and disheartened, Robert grew increasingly stressed and disillusioned with his company. His workday felt more and more like an episode of *Survivor*.

Seeking to improve his performance, Robert enrolled in an executive education program and took the RBS exercise. As part of the exercise, Robert gathered feedback from 11 individuals from his past and present who knew him well. He selected a diverse but balanced group—his wife and two other family members, two friends from his MBA program, two colleagues from his time in the army, and four current colleagues.

Robert then asked these individuals to provide information about his strengths, accompanied by specific examples of moments when Robert used those strengths in ways that were meaningful to them, to their families or teams, or to their organizations. Many people—Robert among them—feel uncomfortable asking for exclusively positive feedback, particularly from colleagues. Accustomed to hearing about their strengths and weaknesses simultaneously,

Requesting Feedback

HERE'S SOME SAMPLE LANGUAGE to use as you solicit feedback from family, friends, teachers, and colleagues.

Dear Colleague,

I'm currently working on creating a personal development plan. As part of that process, I'm gathering feedback from a variety of people I work with closely to help me develop a broader understanding of the strengths I bring to our work. I'm hoping you'll be willing to share your thoughts with me.

From your perspective, what would you say my professional strengths are? Just two or three would be helpful, and if you could cite specific examples of situations where I used those in ways that were meaningful to you, that would be great. Your candid feedback and examples will help me shape my development plan.

Thank you for taking the time to help me.

Sincerely,
X

many executives imagine any positive feedback will be unrealistic, even false. Some also worry that respondents might construe the request as presumptuous or egotistical. But once managers accept that the exercise will help them improve their performance, they tend to dive in.

Within ten days, Robert received e-mail responses from all 11 people describing specific instances when he had made important contributions—including pushing for high quality under a tight deadline, being inclusive in communicating with a diverse group, and digging for critical information. The answers he received surprised him. As a military veteran and a technical person holding an MBA, Robert rarely yielded to his emotions. But in reading story after story from his respondents, Robert found himself deeply moved—as if he were listening to appreciative speeches at a party thrown in his honor. The stories were also surprisingly convincing. He had more strengths than he knew. (For more on Step 1, refer to the sidebar "Gathering Feedback.")

Gathering Feedback

A CRITICAL STEP in the Reflected Best Self exercise involves soliciting feedback from family, friends, teachers, and colleagues. E-mail is an effective way of doing this, not only because it's comfortable and fast but also because it's easy to cut and paste responses into an analysis table such as the one in the main body of this article.

Below is the feedback Robert, a manager we observed, received from a current colleague and from a former coworker in the army.

From: Amy Chen

To: Robert Duggan

Subject: Re: Request for feedback

Dear Robert,

One of the greatest ways that you add value is that you stand for doing the right thing. For example, I think of the time that we were behind on a project for a major client and quality began to slip. You called a meeting and suggested that we had a choice: We could either pull a C by satisfying the basic requirements, or we could pull an A by doing excellent work. You reminded us that we could contribute to a better outcome. In the end, we met our deadline, and the client was very happy with the result.

From: Mike Bruno

To: Robert Duggan

Subject: Re: Request for feedback

One of the greatest ways you add value is that you persist in the face of adversity. I remember the time that we were both leading troops under tight security. We were getting conflicting information from the ground and from headquarters. You pushed to get the ground and HQ folks to talk to each other despite the tight time pressure. That information saved all of our lives. You never lost your calm, and you never stopped expecting or demanding the best from everyone involved.

Step 2: Recognize Patterns

In this step, Robert searched for common themes among the feedback, adding to the examples with observations of his own, then organizing all the input into a table. (To view parts of Robert's table, see the exhibit "Finding common themes.") Like many who participate in the RBS exercise, Robert expected that, given the diversity of respondents, the comments he received would be inconsistent or even competing. Instead, he was struck by their uniformity. The comments from his wife and family members were similar to those

Finding common themes

Creating a table helps you make sense of the feedback you collect. By clustering examples, you can more easily compare responses and identify common themes.

Common theme	Examples given	Possible interpretation
Ethics, values, and courage	• I take a stand when superiors and peers cross the boundaries of ethical behavior. • I am not afraid to stand up for what I believe in. I confront people who litter or who yell at their kids in public.	• I am at my best when I choose the harder right over the easier wrong. I derive even more satisfaction when I am able to teach others. I am professionally courageous.
Curiosity and perseverance	• I gave up a promising career in the military to get my MBA. • I investigated and solved a security breach through an innovative approach.	• I like meeting new challenges. I take risks and persevere despite obstacles.
Ability to build teams	• In high school, I assembled a team of students that helped improve the school's academic standards. • I am flexible and willing to learn from others, and I give credit where credit is due.	• I thrive when working closely with others.

from his army buddies and work colleagues. Everyone took note of Robert's courage under pressure, high ethical standards, perseverance, curiosity, adaptability, respect for diversity, and team-building skills. Robert suddenly realized that even his small, unconscious behaviors had made a huge impression on others. In many cases, he had forgotten about the specific examples cited until he read the feedback, because his behavior in those situations had felt like second nature to him.

The RBS exercise confirmed Robert's sense of himself, but for those who are unaware of their strengths, the exercise can be truly illuminating. Edward, for example, was a recently minted MBA executive in an automotive firm. His colleagues and subordinates were older and more experienced than he, and he felt uncomfortable disagreeing with them. But he learned through the RBS exercise that his peers appreciated his candid alternative views and respected the diplomatic and respectful manner with which he made his assertions. As a result, Edward grew bolder in making the case for his ideas, knowing that his boss and colleagues listened to him, learned from him, and appreciated what he had to say.

Other times, the RBS exercise sheds a more nuanced light on the skills one takes for granted. Beth, for example, was a lawyer who negotiated on behalf of nonprofit organizations. Throughout her life, Beth had been told she was a good listener, but her exercise respondents noted that the interactive, empathetic, and insightful manner in which she listened made her particularly effective. The specificity of the feedback encouraged Beth to take the lead in future negotiations that required delicate and diplomatic communications.

For naturally analytical people, the analysis portion of the exercise serves both to integrate the feedback and develop a larger picture of their capabilities. Janet, an engineer, thought she could study her feedback as she would a technical drawing of a suspension bridge. She saw her "reflected best self" as something to interrogate and improve. But as she read the remarks from family, friends, and colleagues, she saw herself in a broader and more human context. Over time, the stories she read about her enthusiasm and love of design helped her rethink her career path toward more managerial roles in which she might lead and motivate others.

Step 3: Compose Your Self-Portrait

The next step is to write a description of yourself that summarizes and distills the accumulated information. The description should weave themes from the feedback together with your self-observations into a composite of who you are at your best. The self-portrait is not designed to be a complete psychological and cognitive profile. Rather, it should be an insightful image that you can use as a reminder of your previous contributions and as a guide for future action. The portrait itself should not be a set of bullet points but rather a prose composition beginning with the phrase, "When I am at my best, I . . ." The process of writing out a two- to four-paragraph narrative cements the image of your best self in your consciousness. The narrative form also helps you draw connections between the themes in your life that may previously have seemed disjointed or unrelated. Composing the portrait takes time and demands careful consideration, but at the end of this process, you should come away with a rejuvenated image of who you are.

In developing his self-portrait, Robert drew on the actual words that others used to describe him, rounding out the picture with his own sense of himself at his best. He excised competencies that felt off the mark. This didn't mean he discounted them, but he wanted to assure that the overall portrait felt authentic and powerful. "When I am at my best," Robert wrote,

> I stand by my values and can get others to understand why doing so is important. I choose the harder right over the easier wrong. I enjoy setting an example. When I am in learning mode and am curious and passionate about a project, I can work intensely and untiringly. I enjoy taking things on that others might be afraid of or see as too difficult. I'm able to set limits and find alternatives when a current approach is not working. I don't always assume that I am right or know best, which engenders respect from others. I try to empower and give credit to others. I am tolerant and open to differences.

As Robert developed his portrait, he began to understand why he hadn't performed his best at work: He lacked a sense of mission. In the army, he drew satisfaction from the knowledge that the safety of the men and women he led, as well as the nation he served, depended on the quality of his work. He enjoyed the sense of teamwork and variety of problems to be solved. But as an IT manager in charge of routine maintenance on new hardware products, he felt bored and isolated from other people.

The portrait-writing process also helped Robert create a more vivid and elaborate sense of what psychologists would call his "possible self"—not just the person he is in his day-to-day job but the person he might be in completely different contexts. Organizational researchers have shown that when we develop a sense of our best possible self, we are better able to make positive changes in our lives.

Step 4: Redesign Your Job

Having pinpointed his strengths, Robert's next step was to redesign his personal job description to build on what he was good at. Given the fact that routine maintenance work left him cold, Robert's challenge was to create a better fit between his work and his best self. Like most RBS participants, Robert found that the strengths the exercise identified could be put into play in his current position. This involved making small changes in the way he worked, in the composition of his team, and in the way he spent his time. (Most jobs have degrees of freedom in all three of these areas; the trick is operating within the fixed constraints of your job to redesign work at the margins, allowing you to better play to your strengths.)

Robert began by scheduling meetings with systems designers and engineers who told him they were having trouble getting timely information flowing between their groups and Robert's maintenance team. If communication improved, Robert believed, new products would not continue to be saddled with the serious and costly maintenance issues seen in the past. Armed with a carefully documented history of those maintenance problems as well as a new understanding of his naturally analytical and creative team-building skills, Robert began meeting regularly with the designers and engineers to brainstorm better ways to prevent problems with new products. The meetings satisfied two of Robert's deepest best-self needs: He was interacting with more people at work, and he was actively learning about systems design and engineering.

Robert's efforts did not go unnoticed. Key executives remarked on his initiative and his ability to collaborate across functions, as well as on the critical role he played in making new products more reliable. They also saw how he gave credit to others. In less than nine months, Robert's hard work paid off, and he was promoted to program manager. In addition to receiving more pay and higher visibility, Robert enjoyed his work more. His passion was reignited; he felt intensely alive and authentic. Whenever he felt down or lacking in energy, he reread the original e-mail feedback he had received. In difficult situations, the e-mail messages helped him feel more resilient.

Robert was able to leverage his strengths to perform better, but there are cases in which RBS findings conflict with the realities of a person's job. This was true for James, a sales executive who told us he was "in a world of hurt" over his work situation. Unable to meet his ambitious sales goals, tired of flying around the globe to fight fires, his family life on the verge of collapse, James had suffered enough. The RBS exercise revealed that James was at his best when managing people and leading change, but these natural skills did not and could not come into play in his current job. Not long after he did the exercise, he quit his high-stress position and started his own successful company.

Other times, the findings help managers aim for undreamed-of positions in their own organizations. Sarah, a high-level administrator at a university, shared her best-self portrait with key colleagues, asking them to help her identify ways to better exploit her strengths and talents. They suggested that she would be an ideal candidate for a new executive position. Previously, she would never have considered applying for the job, believing herself unqualified. To her surprise, she handily beat out the other candidates.

Beyond Good Enough

We have noted that while people remember criticism, awareness of faults doesn't necessarily translate into better performance. Based on that understanding, the RBS exercise helps you remember your strengths—and construct a plan to build on them. Knowing your strengths also offers you a better understanding of how to deal with your weaknesses—and helps you gain the confidence you need to address them. It allows you to say, "I'm great at leading but lousy at numbers. So rather than teach me remedial math, get me a good finance partner." It also allows you to be clearer in addressing your areas of weakness as a manager. When Tim, a financial services executive, received feedback that he was a great listener and coach, he also became more aware that he had a tendency to spend too much time being a cheerleader and too little time keeping his employees to task. Susan, a senior advertising executive, had the opposite problem: While her feedback lauded her results-oriented management approach, she wanted to be sure that she hadn't missed opportunities to give her employees the space to learn and make mistakes.

In the end, the strength-based orientation of the RBS exercise helps you get past the "good enough" bar. Once you discover who you are at the top of your game, you can use your strengths to better shape the positions you choose to play—both now and in the next phase of your career.

Originally published in January 2005. Reprint R0501G

How to Stay Stuck in the Wrong Career

by Herminia Ibarra

EVERYONE KNOWS A STORY ABOUT A SMART and talented business-person who has lost his or her passion for work, who no longer looks forward to going to the office yet remains stuck without a visible way out. Most everyone knows a story, too, about a person who ditched a 20-year career to pursue something completely different—the lawyer who gave it all up to become a writer or the auditor who quit her accounting firm to start her own toy company—and is the happier for it.

"Am I doing what is right for me, or should I change direction?" is one of the most pressing questions in the mid-career professional's mind today. The numbers of people making major career changes, not to mention those just thinking about it, have risen significantly over the last decade and continue to grow. But the difference between the person who yearns for change yet stays put and the person who takes the leap to find renewed fulfillment at midcareer is not what you might expect. Consider the following examples:

Susan Fontaine made a clean break with her unfulfilling past as partner and head of the strategy practice at a top consulting firm. But the former management consultant—her name, like the names of the other people I studied, has been changed for this article—had not yet had the time to figure out a future direction. When a close client offered her the top strategy job at a *Financial Times* 100 firm, she took it. She was ready for change, and the opportunity was too good to pass up. To her dismay, this position—though perfect according to what she calls "the relentless logic of a post-MBA CV"—was no different from her old job in all the aspects she had been seeking to change. Two weeks into the new role, she realized she had made a terrible mistake.

After a four-week executive education program at a top business school, Harris Roberts, a regulatory affairs director at a major health care firm, was ready for change. He wanted bottom-line responsibility, and he itched to put into practice some of the cutting-edge ideas he had learned in the program. His long-time mentor, the company's CEO, had promised, "When you come back, we'll give you a business unit." But upon Harris's return, a complicated new product introduction delayed the long-awaited transition. He was needed in his old role, so he was asked to postpone his dream. As always, Harris put the company first. But he was disappointed; there was no challenge anymore. Resigned to waiting it out, he created for himself a "network of mentors," senior members of the firm whom he enlisted to guide his development and help him try to land the coveted general management role. Eighteen months later, he was still doing essentially the same job.

A milestone birthday, upheaval in his personal life, and a negative performance evaluation—the first of his career—combined to make a "snapping point" for Gary McCarthy. After business school, the former investment banker and consultant had taken a job at a blue-chip firm by default, biding his time until he found his "true passion." Now, he decided, it was time to make a proactive career choice. Determined to get it right, Gary did all the correct things. He started with a career psychologist who gave him a battery of tests to help him figure out his work interests and values. He talked to headhunters, friends, and family and read bestselling books on career change. By his own account, none of the advice was very useful. He researched possible industries and companies. He made two lists: completely different professions involving things he was passionate about and variations on what he was already doing. A year later, a viable alternative had yet to materialize.

Idea in Brief

Are you one of the growing number of people struggling to make mid-career changes? Searching for ten easy steps to professional reinvention? Or awaiting flashes of insight—while opportunities pass you by?

Would you be willing to jettison all you've heard about career transition and follow a crooked path—rather than the straight and narrow one that's gotten you nowhere?

If so, consider the counterintuitive approach described in this article. It'll have you *doing* instead of infinitely planning. Taking *action* instead of endless self-assessment tests. You'll reinvent your working identity—your sense of who you are as a professional—by experimenting with who you *could* be.

When I consider the experiences of these people and dozens of others I have studied over the past few years, there can be no doubt: Despite the rhetoric, a true change of direction is very hard to swing. This isn't because managers or professionals are typically unwilling to change; on the contrary, many make serious attempts to reinvent themselves, devoting large amounts of time and energy to the process at great professional and personal risk. But despite heroic efforts, they remain stuck in the wrong careers, not living up to their potential and sacrificing professional fulfillment.

Many academics and career counselors observe this inertia and conclude that the problem lies in basic human motives: We fear change, lack readiness, are unwilling to make sacrifices, sabotage ourselves. My in-depth research (see the sidebar "Studying Career Change" for an explanation of my methods) leads me to a different conclusion: People most often fail because they go about it all wrong. Indeed, the conventional wisdom on how to change careers is in fact a prescription for how to stay put. The problem lies in our methods, not our motives.

In my study, I saw many people try a conventional approach and then languish for months, if not years. But by taking a different tack, one I came to call the practice of *working identity*, they eventually found their way to brand-new careers. The phrase "working identity," of course, carries two meanings. It is, first, our sense of self in our professional roles, what we convey about ourselves to others

Idea in Practice

Sounds Reasonable, But . . .

Consider the traditional "plan and implement" approach to career change: Assess your interests, skills, and experience; identify appropriate jobs; consult friends, colleagues, career counselors; take the plunge.

This all *sounds* reasonable—but it actually fosters stagnation. You get mired in introspection while searching for your "one true self" a futile quest, since individuals have many possible selves. Your ideal won't necessarily find a match in the real world. Worse, this method encourages making a big change all at once—which can land you in the wrong job.

Sounds Crazy, But . . .

Now consider the "test and learn" method: You put *several*

working identities into practice, refining them until they're sufficiently grounded in experience to inspire more decisive steps. You make your possible *future* working identities vivid, tangible, and compelling—countering the tendency to grab familiar work when the unknown becomes too scary.

Reinventing your working identity takes several years—and may land you in surprising places. But that doesn't mean the process must be random. These tactics provide a method to the seeming madness:

- Craft experiments. Play with new professional roles on a limited but tangible scale, without compromising your current job. Try freelance assignments or pro bono work. Moonlight. Use sabbaticals or

and, ultimately, how we live our working lives. But it can also denote action—a process of applying effort to reshape that identity. Working our identity, I found, is a matter of skill, not personality, and therefore can be learned by almost anyone seeking professional renewal. But first we have to be willing to abandon everything we have ever been taught about making sound career decisions.

A Three-Point Plan

We like to think that the key to a successful career change is knowing what we want to do next, then using that knowledge to guide our actions. But studying people in the throes of the career change process (as opposed to afterward, when hindsight is always 20/20) led extended vacations to explore new directions.

Example: A former investment banker dabbled in wine tours and scuba diving businesses before determining that such work wouldn't hold his interest long-term. Realizing a "more normal" career path would better serve his emotional and financial needs, he is now a internal venture capitalist for a media company.

- Shift connections. Strangers can best help you see who you're becoming, providing fresh ideas uncolored by your previous identity. Make new connections by working for people you've long admired and can learn from. Find people—perhaps through alumni and company networks—who can help you grow into your possible new selves.

- Make sense. Infuse events with special meaning. Weave them into a story about who you're becoming. Relate that story publicly. You'll clarify your intentions, stay motivated, and inspire others' support.

Example: An investment banker considering fiction writing visited an astrologer, who noted that forces pulling him in opposing directions (stability versus creative expression) were irreconcilable. He told everyone this story and wrote about it in his local newspaper. The more he communicated it, the more the incident made sense—and the more friends and family supported his writing ambitions.

me to a startling conclusion: Change actually happens the other way around. Doing comes first, knowing second.

Why? Because changing careers means redefining our working identity. Career change follows a first-act-and-then-think sequence because who we are and what we do are tightly connected, the result of years of action; to change that connection, we must also resort to action—exactly what the conventional wisdom cautions us against.

Conventional career change methods—Susan's "logical" CV progression, Harris's networking, and Gary's planning—are all part of what I call the "plan and implement" model of change. It goes like this: First, determine with as much clarity and certainty as possible what you really want to do. Next, use that knowledge to identify jobs or fields in which your passions can be coupled with your skills and

Studying Career Change

CERTAIN CAREER TRANSITIONS HAVE BEEN thoroughly studied and are well understood: a move into a position of greater managerial responsibility and organizational status, a transfer to a similar job in a new company or industry, a lateral move into a different work function within a familiar field. But few researchers have investigated how managers and professionals go about making a true change of direction.

My research is an in-depth study of 39 people who changed, or were in the process of trying to change, careers. Determining the magnitude of any work transition is highly subjective. Who, apart from the person who has lived through it, can say whether a shift is radical or incremental? After interviewing dozens of people who were making very different kinds of career moves, I settled on a three-part definition of career change.

Some of the people in my study made significant changes in the context in which they worked, most typically jumping from large, established companies to small, entrepreneurial organizations or to self-employment or between the for-profit and nonprofit sectors. Others made major changes in the content of the work, sometimes leaving occupations, such as medicine, law or academia, that they had trained for extensively. The majority made significant changes in both what they did and where they did it, but most

experience. Seek advice from the people who know you best and from professionals in tune with the market. Then simply implement the resulting action steps. Change is seen as a one-shot deal: The plan-and-implement approach cautions us against making a move before we know exactly where we are going.

It all sounds reasonable, and it is a reassuring way to proceed. Yet my research suggests that proceeding this way will lead to the most disastrous of results, which is to say no result. So if your deepest desire is to remain indefinitely in a career that grates on your nerves or stifles your self-expression, simply adhere to that conventional wisdom, presented below as a foolproof, three-point plan.

Know Thyself

Like Gary McCarthy, most of us are taught to begin a career change with a quest for self-knowledge. Knowing, in theory, comes from self-reflection, in solitary introspection or with the help of standard-

important, all experienced a feeling of having reached a crossroad, one that would require psychological change.

My sample ranged in age from 32 to 51, with an average of 41. I chose this range not to coincide with the infamous midlife crisis but to study a group of people with enough experience in one career to make a shift to another high-stakes endeavor. Sixty-five percent of the participants were men. Almost half of the subjects lived and worked outside the United States, mostly in France and the UK. It was a highly credentialed sample: All had college degrees, and about three-fourths held graduate or professional degrees (business, science, law, and so on). They represented all walks of managerial and professional life, including business management, law, finance, academia, medicine, science, and technology.

Some of the interviews were retrospective, with people who had already completed their changes. With people at earlier stages of the transition, I conducted an average of three interviews over two to three years. The interviews were open-ended, typically beginning with: "Tell me about your career to date." Between the interviews, I had e-mail exchanges and telephone conversations with participants to keep track of their progress. I supplemented this core study with many shorter interviews involving a range of career change professionals, including headhunters, venture capitalists, career counselors, and outplacement specialists.

ized questionnaires and certified professionals. Learning whether we are introverted or extroverted, whether we prefer to work in a structured and methodical environment or in chaos, whether we place greater value on impact or income helps us avoid jobs that will again prove unsatisfying. Having reached an understanding of his or her temperament, needs, competencies, core values, and priorities, a person can go out and find a job or organization that matches.

Gary did all these things. Armed with his test results, he researched promising companies and industries and networked with a lot of people to get leads and referrals. He made two lists of possibilities: "conformist" and "nonconformist." But what happened from there, and what consumed 90% of the year he spent looking for a new career, is what the conventional models leave out—a lot of trial and error.

Gary started with several rounds of talking with traditional companies and headhunters. Next, he tried to turn a passion or a hobby into a career: He and his wife wrote a business plan for a wine-tour business. The financials were not great, so they dropped it. Next,

Our Many Possible Selves

WHAT IS IDENTITY? MOST TRADITIONAL DEFINITIONS—the ones that form the foundation for most career advice—are based on the notion of an "inner core" or a "true self." By early adulthood, these theories suggest, a person has formed a relatively stable personality structure, defined by his or her aptitudes, preferences, and values. Excavating this true self—often forgotten in a dead-end pursuit of fame, fortune, or social approval—should be the starting point of any career reorientation, according to conventional wisdom. With the appropriate self-knowledge, obtained via introspection and psychological testing, a person can more easily search for the right "match" and avoid the mistakes of the past. This true-self definition corresponds perfectly to the plan-and-implement method—once we find the self, all that remains is execution.

The work of Stanford cognitive psychologist Hazel Markus and other behavioral scientists, however, offers a different definition of identity, one that is more consistent with what I have discovered: We are many selves. And while these selves are defined partly by our histories, they are defined just as powerfully by our present circumstances and our hopes and fears for the future.

Our possible selves—the images and fantasies we all have about who we hope to become, think we should become, or even fear becoming—are at the heart of the career change process. Although conventional wisdom says pain—a self we fear becoming—is the only driver for change, in reality pain can create paralysis. We change only when we have enticing alternatives that we can feel, touch, and taste. That is why working identity, as a practice,

---

he pursued his true fantasy career: Gary got certified as a scuba instructor and looked into the purchase of a dive operation. He soon learned, though, that his dream job was unlikely to hold his interest over the long term (and thus was not worth the economic sacrifice). So he went back to the headhunters and traditional companies, only to reconfirm that he did not want what they had to offer. Next, he identified entrepreneurs he admired and looked for ways to get his foot in their doors. He explored freelancing, trying to get short-term projects in exciting young companies. But a precise match did not materialize.

Certainly the common practice of looking back over our careers and identifying what we liked and disliked, what we found satisfying and not satisfying, can be a useful tool. But too often this

is necessarily a process of experimenting, testing, and learning about our possible selves.

Take Gary McCarthy, the former investment banker and consultant profiled in the main article. The set of possible selves he considered is typical in its number and range. It included a "ditch it all and open a tour-guide business in the south of France with my wife" self; a socially respectable "junior part-ner" self that his parents would have endorsed; a youthful, outdoorsy, "follow your passion" self who renounced convention and wanted to open a scuba business; a "responsible spouse and future parent" self who wanted to make good dual-career decisions; a "corporate drone at age 50, full of regrets" self; an "apprentice" self who learned at the elbow of an admired entrepreneur; and a practical, reasonable, "go to a traditional company where I can com-bine my backgrounds in banking and consulting" self.

Conventional wisdom would say that the scope of his list of possibilities was evidence that he lacked focus and wasn't ready for change. But within the working identity framework, it was precisely this variety that allowed him to find a truly good fit. Certain possible selves are concrete and tangible, defined by the things we do and the company we keep today; others remain vague and fuzzy, existing only in the realm of private dreams, hypothetical possibilities, and abstract ideas. By bringing the possibilities—both desired and feared, present and future—more sharply into focus, we give ourselves a concrete base of experience from which to choose among them.

practice is rooted in the profound misconception that it is possible to discover one's "true self," when the reality is that none of us has such an essence. (See the sidebar "Our Many Possible Selves" for a discussion of why one's true self is so elusive.) Intense introspection also poses the danger that a potential career changer will get stuck in the realm of daydreams. Either the fantasy never finds a match in a real-world, paycheck-producing job or, unlike Gary, we remain emotionally attached to a fantasy career that we do not realize we have outgrown.

We learn who we have become—in practice, not in theory—by testing fantasy and reality, not by "looking inside." Knowing one-self is crucial, but it is usually the outcome of—and not a first input to—the reinvention process. Worse, starting out by trying to identify one's true self often causes paralysis. While we wait for the flash of blinding insight, opportunities pass us by. To launch ourselves anew, we need to get out of our heads. We need to *act*.

Consult Trusted Advisers

If you accept the conventional wisdom that career change begins with self-knowledge and proceeds through an objective scrutiny of the available choices, who should you turn to for guidance? Conventional wisdom has it that you should look to those who know you best and those who know the market. Friends and family—with whom you share a long history—can offer insight into your true nature, and they have your best interests at heart; professionals add a dose of pragmatism, keeping you grounded in the realities of the marketplace.

In times of change and uncertainty, we naturally take comfort in our enduring connections with friends and family. But when it comes to reinventing ourselves, the people who know us best are the ones most likely to hinder rather than help us. They may wish to be supportive, but they tend to reinforce—or even desperately try to preserve—the old identities we are trying to shed. Early in his career, Gary discovered that his close circle would not be much help. "I wanted to do something different but was shocked to realize that people were already pigeonholing me," he says. "I tried to brainstorm with friends and family about what other things I might do. All the ideas that came back were a version of 'Well, you could get a middle management job in a finance department of a company.' Or 'You could become a trainee in a management program.'" John Alexander, an investment banker hoping to make a go of fiction writing, reports that he had often discussed his career predicament with his friends and family. "They would tend to say, 'I can see why writing might be interesting, but you've got a very good job, and do you really want to jeopardize that?'"

Mentors and close coworkers, though well meaning, can also unwittingly hold us back. Take Harris Roberts, the health care company director who wanted to assume a general management role. The people around him, who were invested in his staying put, only mirrored his normal doubts about moving outside his comfort zone.

His mentors cared about him and held the power to make his desired change a reality. But they made a fence, not a gateway, blocking the moves that would lead to career change. By talking only to people who inhabited his immediate professional world, people whose ideas for him didn't go beyond the four walls, Harris seriously limited himself. Not only did he lack outside market information, but these coworkers could no more let go of their outdated image of a junior Harris than he himself could.

Headhunters and outplacers, today's career change professionals, can keep us tethered to the past just as effectively. We assume, rightly, that they have the market perspective we lack—but we forget that they are in the business of facilitating incremental moves along an established trajectory. At midcareer, however, many people are no longer looking to "leverage past experience in a different setting." They want to invent their own jobs and escape the shackles of corporate convention, in some cases to do something completely different. What Susan Fontaine, the management consultant, experienced is typical: "I found headhunters unhelpful, basically. I would say, 'Here are my skills; what else might I do?' And they kept saying, 'Why don't you move to Andersen?' or, 'Why don't you try Bain?' All they could suggest was exactly the same thing. I kept saying, 'I'm quite clear I don't want to do that, and if I did want to do that, I would not come to you. I can do that on my own.'"

So if self-assessment, the advice of close ones, and the counsel of change professionals won't do it, then where can we find support for our reinvention? To make a true break with the past, we need to see ourselves in a new light. We need guides who have been there and can understand where we are going. Reaching outside our normal circles to new people, networks, and professional communities is the best way to both break frame and get psychological sustenance.

Think Big

We like to think that we can leap directly from a desire for change to a single decision that will complete our reinvention—the conventional wisdom would say you shouldn't fool yourself with small, superficial adjustments. But trying to tackle the big changes too quickly can be counterproductive. Just as starting the transition by looking for one's true self can cause paralysis rather than progress, trying to make one big move once and for all can prevent real change.

When Susan Fontaine decided to leave her consulting career, it was with good reason. A single mother of two, she was finding the travel and other demands on her personal life increasingly intolerable. She quit her job and resolved to spend some time exploring her options. That resolve vanished, however, when financial pressure coincided with a flattering offer to join the management team of a former client. She accepted the new position only to discover that its demands would be very similar to those of the position she had left. "I thought, 'What have I done?'" she later told me. "I had had the opportunity to leave all that!" By hoping to solve all her problems in one fell swoop, Susan made a change that amounted to no change at all. Two weeks into the new job, she resigned.

As much as we might want to avoid endless procrastination, premature closure is not the answer. It takes time to discover what we truly want to change and to identify the deeply grooved habits and assumptions that are holding us back. The lesson of Susan's story is that trying to make a single bold move can bring us back to square one all too quickly. A longer, less linear transition process may leave us feeling that we are wasting time. But as we will see below, taking smaller steps can allow a richer, more grounded redefinition of our working identity to emerge.

Three Success Stories

Although they floundered, victims of conventional wisdom, Gary McCarthy, Harris Roberts, and Susan Fontaine eventually moved on to a different—and more successful—approach. Gary is now at a media company he admires, working as an internal venture capitalist, a role that allows him to use his skill set in consulting and finance but grants him great creative latitude and total ownership of his results. Harris is president and COO of a growing medical device company and very much involved in setting the strategic direction of his new firm. Susan is working with nonprofits, bringing her strategy expertise to this sector and loving her work.

None of them followed a straight and narrow route. Gary dabbled in wine tours and flirted with buying a scuba diving operation before settling on what his wife called a more normal path. Harris had his prized general management role snatched from under him a second time as the result of a corporate restructuring. He considered leaving for a biotech start-up but realized that he simply did not have the appetite for such a risky move. Susan set up temporarily as a freelance consultant, landing traditional consulting projects to pay the bills and using her discretionary time to explore a more varied portfolio of assignments.

Their experience is typical. Nearly everyone who tries to figure out a next career takes a long time to find the one that is truly right. Most career transitions take about three years. It is rarely a linear path: We take two steps forward and one step back, and where we end up often surprises us.

Working Identity

Once we start questioning not just whether we are in the right job or organization today but also what we thought we wanted for the future, the job search methods we have all been taught fail us. But that doesn't mean we must resign ourselves to a random process governed by factors outside our control—life crisis that forces us to reprioritize, an unexpected job offer. There is an alternative method that works according to a different logic than the plan-and-implement approach. Gary, Harris, and Susan, as well as many other successful career changers I have observed, shared this method, which I call the "test and learn" model of change. During times of transition—when our possible selves are shifting wildly—the only way to create change is by putting our possible identities into practice, working and crafting them until they are sufficiently grounded in experience to guide more decisive steps. (See the sidebar "Test and Learn.")

The test-and-learn approach recognizes that the only way to counter uncertainty and resist the pull of the familiar is to make alternative futures more vivid, more tangible, and more doable. We acquired our old identities in practice. Likewise, we redefine them, in practice, by crafting experiments, shifting connections, and making sense of the changes we are going through. These three common practices lie at the heart of the most disparate of career changes, lending logic to what can look like chance occurrences and disorderly behavior.

Crafting experiments

By far the biggest mistake people make when trying to change careers is delaying the first step until they have settled on a destination. This error is undermining because the only way we figure out what we really want to do is by giving it a try. Understandably, most people are reluctant to leap into the unknown. We must test our fantasies—otherwise, they remain just that. I discovered that most people create new working identities on the side at first, by getting involved in extracurricular ventures and weekend projects.

Crafting experiments refers to the practice of creating these side projects. Their great advantage is that we can try out new professional roles on a limited scale without compromising our current jobs or having to leap into new positions too quickly. In almost every instance of successful change that I have observed, the person had already been deeply engaged in the new career for quite some time.

There are many ways to set up experiments that work. Newly resolved to explore a range of possibilities, Susan took freelancing assignments in her old line of work and did pro bono work for charities as her lifeline to get her through this difficult period. Through that work, she began to develop contacts that led to paid charity consulting. Gradually, she became immersed in nonprofits, a sector she had never expected to find a career in. And she found herself enjoying freelancing. Today, she is working with the largest UK consulting firm that specializes in charities, and she has this to say: "All I hope is that I never again make the mistake of jumping before giving myself the chance to explore what I really want to do."

Test and Learn

YOUR WORKING IDENTITY IS an amalgam of the kind of work you do, the relationships and organizations that form part of your work life, and the story you tell about why you do what you do and how you arrived at that point. Reshaping that identity, therefore, is a matter of making adjustments to all three of those aspects over time. The adjustments happen tentatively and incrementally, so the process can seem disorderly. In fact, it is a logical process of testing, discovering, and adapting that can be learned by almost anyone seeking professional renewal.

Crafting experiments

Working identity is defined by what we do, the professional activities that engage us.	►	Try out new activities and professional roles on a small scale before making a major commitment to a different path.

Shifting connections

Working identity is also defined by the company we keep, our working relationships, and the professional groups to which we belong.	►	Develop contacts that can open doors to new worlds, and look for role models and new reference groups to guide and benchmark your progress.

Making sense

Working identity is also defined by the formative events in our lives and the stories that link who we were and who we will become.	►	Find or create catalysts and triggers for change, and use them as occasions to rework your life story.

Other people use temporary assignments, outside contracts, advisory work, and moonlighting to get experience or build skills in new industries. Thanks to a temporary stint at the helm of his division, Harris got over his fear, which had silently plagued him for years, that he lacked the finance and cross-functional background necessary to be a good general manager. This concrete experience, more than any amount of self-reflection, helped him envision himself as a general manager. Taking courses or picking up training and credentials in a new area is still another way of experimenting. For many of the people in my study, an executive program, sabbatical, or extended vacation improved their capacity to move in a new direction. These breaks are powerful because they force us to step back from the daily routine while engaging us with new people and activities.

Shifting connections

Consider how common it is for employees to say of their companies, "There is no one here I want to be like." At midcareer, our desire for change is rarely about only the work we do; it is perhaps more importantly about changing our working relationships so they are more satisfying and inspiring. Shifting connections refers to the practice of finding people who can help us see and grow into our new selves. For most successful career changers I have observed, a guiding figure or new professional community helped to light the way and cushion the eventual leap.

Finding a new job always requires networking outside our usual circles. We get ideas and job leads by branching out. Gary, for example, used his alumni and company networks quite successfully. It was an ex-employee of his company—someone he didn't know personally—who got him the temporary project at his current company. But what clinched his decision, what made this job different from all the other conformist roles he had considered, was the opportunity to work for a role model he had long admired and from whom he could learn the ropes.

Seeking refuge in close working relationships is natural in times of change and uncertainty. But Harris made a classic mistake in turning to an old mentor, Alfred, who was too invested in Harris remaining the unsure protégé to give him room to grow. Harris's way out of this "codependent" relationship came via a person he had met casually at a professional conference. Gerry, the company founder who later hired Harris as his COO, initially approached Harris for regulatory advice. Eventually, they developed an informal consulting relationship. In Gerry, Harris found a person who believed in his potential as a general manager and offered a different kind of close, interdependent working relationship: "It was such a contrast to my relationship with Alfred," Harris says. "It's not as paternal. Gerry knows things I need to learn—things that relate to creative financing, ways to raise money—but he also needs to learn from me. He doesn't know how to run a company, and I do. He's looking to me to teach him what's necessary to develop an organization, to build a foundation. I think I can learn a lot from Gerry, but it's a more mature and more professional relationship than I had with Alfred."

To make a break with the past, we must venture into unknown networks—and not just for job leads. Often it is strangers who are best equipped to help us see who we are becoming.

Making sense

In the middle of the confusion about which way to go, many of us hope for one event that will clarify everything, that will transform our stumbling moves into a coherent trajectory. Julio Gonzales, a doctor trying to leave the practice of medicine, put it like this: "I was waiting for an epiphany—I wake up in the middle of the night and the Angel of Mercy tells me *this* is what I should do." The third working identity practice, making sense, refers to creating our own triggers for change: infusing events—the momentous and the mundane— with special meaning and weaving them into a story about who we are becoming.

Every person who has changed careers has a story about the moment of truth. For John Alexander, the would-be author I've mentioned, the moment of truth came when, on a whim, he visited an astrologer. To his surprise, the first thing she said to him was, "I'm glad I haven't been *you* for the last two or three years. You have been undergoing a painful internal tug-of-war between two opposing factions. One side wants stability, economic well-being, and social status, and the other craves artistic expression, maybe as a writer or an impresario. You may wish to believe that there can be reconciliation between these two. I tell you, there cannot be." Another career changer, a woman who had grown increasingly frustrated as an executive in a high-tech start-up, said, "One day my husband just asked me, 'Are you happy? If you are, that's great. But you don't *look* happy.' His question prompted me to reconsider what I was doing."

It would be easy to believe from such accounts that career changes have their geneses in such moments. But the moment of insight is an effect, not a cause, of change. Across my many interviews, a striking discovery was that such moments tended to occur late in the transition process, only after much trial and tribulation. Rather than catalyzing change, defining moments helped people make sense of changes that had long been unfolding.

Trigger events don't just jolt us out of our habitual routines, they are the necessary pegs on which to hang our reinvention stories. Arranging life events into a coherent story is one of the subtlest, yet most demanding, challenges of career reinvention. To reinvent oneself is to rework one's story. At the start of a career transition, when all we have is a laundry list of diffuse ideas, it unsettles us that we have no story. It disturbs us to find so many different options appealing, and we worry that the same self who once chose what we no longer want to do might again make a bad choice. Without a story that explains why we must change, the external audience to whom we are selling our reinvention remains dubious, and we, too, feel unsettled and uncertain.

Good stories develop in the telling and retelling, by being put into the public sphere even before they are fully formed. Instead of being embarrassed about having visited an astrologer, for example, John told everyone his story and even wrote about it in a newspaper column. The closer he got to finding his creative outlet, the more the episode made sense and the less often his story elicited the "Why would you want to do that?" reaction. By making public declarations about what we seek and about the common thread that binds our old and new selves, we clarify our intentions and improve our ability to enlist others' support.

The Road Now Taken

Most of us know what we are trying to escape: the lockstep of a narrowly defined career, inauthentic or unstimulating work, numbing corporate politics, a lack of time for life outside of work. Finding an alternative that truly fits, like finding one's mission in life, cannot be accomplished overnight. It takes time, perseverance, and hard work. But effort isn't enough; a sound method and the skill to put it into practice are also required.

The idea of working one's identity flies in the face of everything we have always been told about choosing careers. It asks us to devote the greater part of our time and energy to action rather than reflection, to doing instead of planning. It tells us to give up the search for a ten-point plan and to accept instead a crooked path. But what appears to be a mysterious, road-to-Damascus process is actually a learning-by-doing practice that any of us can adopt. We start by taking action.

Originally published in December 2002. Reprint R0212B

Reinventing Your Career in a Time of Crisis

by Herminia Ibarra

Unexpected events or shocks disrupt our habitual routines, jolt us out of our comfort zones, and lead us to ask big questions about what matters and what is worth doing. It's no wonder, then, that during a crisis such as the coronavirus pandemic, many people are rethinking their careers.

But how do we balance the pressing need to ensure basic survival—of our families and firms—with what may well be a growing urge to do something new after the crisis has subsided?

I've been studying career change for the past two decades, a period that has spanned the dot-com boom and bust, the 2008 financial crisis, the subsequent extended bull-market run, and now the Covid-19 pandemic that has brought that run to an end. My experience has taught me that a few simple principles can help those living through hard times continue to focus on reinventing their careers.

Develop Many Possible Selves

When you don't know what the future will bring, or when the path you thought you were on takes an unexpected turn, it makes sense to pursue a diverse portfolio of options rather than just sticking single-mindedly to one. Even in happier times, career change is never a perfectly linear process. It's a necessarily messy journey of exploration—and to do it right, you have to experiment with, test, and learn about a range of possible selves.

Possible selves are the ideas we all have about who we might want to become. Some are concrete and well-informed by experience; others are vague and fuzzy, nascent and untested. Some are realistic; others are pure fantasy. And, naturally, some appeal more to us than others.

Today more than ever, the path to your next career will be circuitous. To cover all the ground you'll need to cover, it's vital to let yourself imagine a divergent set of possible selves and futures. Embrace that process and explore as many of them as you can.

Embrace the "Liminal" Period

The hallmark of the career-change process is the emotional experience of "liminality"—that is, of existing between a past that is clearly gone and a future that is still uncertain. Liminality can be an unpleasant state to inhabit emotionally. People going through it feel unmoored, lose their bearings, and oscillate between "holding on" and "letting go." But this fraught stage is a necessary part of the journey, because it allows you to process a lot of complex emotions and conflicting desires and ultimately prevents you from shutting down prematurely and missing better options that still lie ahead.

A crisis is likely to prolong this state of liminality for many of us. While frustrating at times, it has its benefits. As Bill Bridges has written in *Transitions*, "We need not feel defensive about this apparently unproductive time-out at turning points in our lives. . . . In the apparently aimless activity of our time alone, we are doing important inner business."

Neurological studies suggest that taking advantage of liminal time to do that "inner business" may be more beneficial than engaging in a flurry of busy-making self-improvement efforts. Downtime is crucial not only for replenishing the brain's stores of attention and motivation but also for sustaining the cognitive processes that allow us to fully develop our humanity. It's how we consolidate memories, integrate what we've learned, plan for the future, maintain our moral compass, and construct our sense of ourselves.

Get Going on Projects

The most common path to a career reinvention involves doing something on the side—cultivating knowledge, skills, resources, and relationships until you've got strong new legs to walk on in exploring a new career. On nights and weekends, people take part-time courses, do pro bono or advisory work, and develop start-up ideas. In the research I did for my book *Working Identity*, which is devoted to the subject of career reinvention, I found that most people work on several possibilities at once, comparing and contrasting the pros and cons of each. This activity is crucial. It helps you work through not only the practical questions but also the existential ones that drive career change: Who am I? Who do I want to become? Where can I best contribute? We learn who we want to become by testing fantasy and reality, and, of course, by *doing*.

The conditions of a crisis (such as lockdown during the coronavirus pandemic) limit the possibilities, of course. People have long used contract or advisory work to explore new options or to finance new ventures, for example, but nonessential budgets often dry up when the economy contracts, and as a result many people find these avenues closed to them.

Nevertheless, under such circumstances (think of widespread self-quarantining) many people find it easier than before to reallocate time and resources to back-burner projects and take advantage of the moment. As part of a webinar I teach on career reinvention, I conducted an online poll asking participants to describe how they're responding to the coronavirus crisis, and 50% of the 2,000 people who responded reported that it has given them "opportunities to try new things or learn new skills." In some cases, these new skills are directly related to working remotely. That's certainly been the case for me: Like most of my faculty colleagues, I've had to quickly learn to teach online.

You don't need to limit your projects to the domain of your desired career change. Many people today are doing rewarding work and making surprising discoveries by engaging in crisis initiatives at their organizations or in community volunteer efforts. The point is to do new and different work with new and different people, because that process represents an opportunity to learn about yourself, your likes and dislikes, and the social contexts and kinds of people that bring out the best in you.

Work Your "Dormant" Ties

Networking is a contact sport, which makes it hard to play in a lock-down. How can you initiate and build the relationships you need in order to reinvent yourself with people who may be struggling to adapt to difficult circumstances themselves?

The golden rule of networking for career change has always been to mobilize your weak ties—that is, the relationships you have with people you don't know very well or don't see very often, in order to maximize your chances of learning things you don't already know. The problem with friends, family, and close coworkers—your strong ties—is that they know the same things you know. They'll want to help you, of course, but they're unlikely to be able to think creatively about your future. However well-intentioned they are, they tend to pigeonhole you.

But there's a catch when it comes to your weak ties. Although these people are more likely to be a source of useful new information and resources, they're also likely to be less motivated to help you, especially when they're stretched themselves. For this reason, in times of uncertainty people rely more on their strong ties, which are based on commitment, trust, and obligation.

One way around this weak tie/strong tie conundrum is to make use of your "dormant ties"—the relationships with people you were once close to but haven't been in contact with for roughly three years or more. In one study, more than 200 executives were asked to reconnect with such people and to use their interactions to get information or advice that might help them on an important work project. The executives reported that the advice they received from these dormant sources was on average more valuable and novel than what they obtained from their more-active relationships.

Talk It Out

In the middle of the confusion that career change can bring, many of us hope that introspection will eventually produce a flash of insight. But as I learned during the research phase of my book *Working Identity*, solitary introspection, when not coupled with active experimentation, is dangerous, because it can lead us to get stuck in the realm of daydreams—which, of course, provide neither gainful employment nor career fulfillment.

Self-reflection, paradoxically, is a practice best nourished by talking out loud in social exchanges with people who respond, sympathize, commiserate, question, read your body language, and share their own experiences. One of the reasons potential career changers benefit so much from attending courses is that their fellow students represent a ready-made community of kindred spirits to talk to. Just the simple act of committing yourself publicly to the idea of reinventing your career—by creating and telling a story about what you want to do or why you want a change—can clarify your thinking and propel you forward. And any veteran storyteller will tell you that there's no substitute for practicing in front of a live audience.

Doing this during a crisis may require a bit more initiative and creativity than usual, but even with the self-isolation and social distancing of Covid-19, you can find ways to test your ideas out loud— by scheduling walks at a safe distance, by working with a career coach online, or by creating a video conference group that meets regularly to share plans.

In the end, when it comes to reinventing your career in a time of crisis, remember this important point: The time to get going is now—but don't go it alone.

Adapted from content originally published on April 27, 2020. Reprint #HO5L2N

Five Ways to Bungle a Job Change

by Boris Groysberg and Robin Abrahams

THE AVERAGE BABY BOOMER will switch jobs 10 times, according to the U.S. Bureau of Labor Statistics. The worker as free agent—a concept popularized in the 1990s—remains a reality regardless of economic conditions, making it incumbent on all of us to take greater control of our own careers. The corporate ladder is still being disassembled like a Jenga tower, and even the CEO position is no longer a terminus. As one independent financier we interviewed put it, "[T]here are no final destinations. [Your career] is a process of continuous development."

But while job moves are just about inevitable, they are seldom easy and nearly always emotionally fraught—and too often they lead to a noticeable decline in performance, in both the short and the long term. For instance, in previous research we found that star equities analysts moving to new investment banks experienced drops in performance that lasted as long as five years. People who switch organizations—whether they're wide receivers changing football teams or general managers going to new companies—all face similar problems. It's not just about the learning curve. Moves of all kinds entail significant internal and external challenges and transaction costs: upheaval in your home and social life; potential relocation expenses; adjustments to new cultural and political norms; navigation of unclear expectations; and the need to learn a new canon, skill set, and jargon.

Debating the merits of a particular offer might seem like a luxury when jobs are scarce. And of course there are times when you have no choice but to accept a less-than-perfect fit for financial reasons. Even so, a job is never just a job. This is your *career* we're talking about. The occasional misstep can be forgiven, but a careful and conscious assessment of the risks and realities will help you avoid making too many mistakes or ones that amount to a major setback.

The Most Common Missteps

To identify the most frequent job-hopping errors, we analyzed data from three research streams: a survey of executive search consultants, a survey of HR heads at multinational companies, and interviews with C-level executives around the world. (See the sidebar "About Our Research.")

The job-change mistakes we outline in this article are by far the ones most commonly cited by the search consultants; the themes are echoed in the HR heads' survey comments and in the executives' stories about their best and worst decisions. The mistakes are: not doing enough research, leaving for money, going "from" rather than "to," overestimating yourself, and thinking short term. They follow predictable patterns and persist throughout the course of a career.

These mistakes are not independent of one another; they play out as a system of maladaptive behaviors, dissatisfaction, unrealistic hopes, ill-considered moves, and more dissatisfaction. Fixating on money, for instance, can obscure the need for research. Overestimating yourself can cause you to ignore a bad fit—a problem that research might have helped you anticipate. Some job seekers make all five mistakes at once: Because they overvalue themselves, they feel unjustly treated at year-end review time and leave for the first company that promises a signing bonus, without doing due diligence on the firm's long-term prospects.

The executives we surveyed and spoke to were not young, untested managers. We zeroed in on seasoned individuals (mostly in the C-suite) with substantial experience making hiring decisions of their own at the very highest levels. But, as one search consultant

Idea in Brief

The average baby boomer switches jobs 10 times in his or her career. Though such moves are just about inevitable, they're seldom easy and they often lead to a noticeable decline in both short- and long-term performance. That's because people make them for the wrong reasons. Drawing on an extensive survey of executive search consultants, as well as surveys of HR heads and interviews with C-level executives around the world, the authors have identified senior managers' five most common career missteps: not doing enough research, leaving for money, going "from" rather than "to," overestimating yourself, and thinking short term. These mistakes follow predictable patterns and persist throughout the course of a career; they're often a direct result of psychological, social, and time pressures. What if you do take the wrong job? The authors' research indicates that you should cut your losses and leave. But fleeing to another bad situation is not the answer. Make your next move strategically—and wherever you are in the search process, don't hesitate to go down another road when it becomes evident that a certain kind of change wouldn't be right.

reminded us, many successful people haven't looked for a job for years—sometimes decades—and thus are surprisingly ignorant about job-market realities. In the words of another consultant, "They assume that companies will be as flexible about having them learn new areas of business as they were when they were young." They have unrealistic expectations about how long it will take to find a job, and if they're high up in the hierarchy, it may have been some time since they received truly honest feedback about their strengths and weaknesses. That's one reason they stumble into such predictable traps. (The blame doesn't fall solely on the recruits, though. Companies chase these stars, hoping to simply plug them into an existing org chart. Too often, they are minimally strategic in their selection and even less strategic in integrating their new hires.)

Mistake 1: Not doing enough research

Search consultants told us that job hunters neglect due diligence in four important areas.

About Our Research

FOR THIS ARTICLE, WE CONDUCTED a survey of 400 executive search consultants from more than 50 industries, interviews with more than 500 C-level executives in 40 countries, and a survey of HR heads at 15 multinational companies.

The search consultants had extensive experience placing the best and brightest: In our sample, 67% had 10-plus years of experience, and 70% recruited for stars at the senior-executive level or higher. We asked the consultants to name the most common mistakes people make when contemplating a job change and the reasons for those mistakes. We posed similar questions to the HR heads. The interviews with executives were conducted by students in Boris Groysberg's 2008 class Managing Human Capital.

The consultants referred to a total of 738 mistakes. The top five kinds discussed in this article represent nearly two-thirds of them: We had 127 references to not doing enough research, 117 to leaving for money, 104 to going "from" rather than "to," 76 to overestimating yourself, and 60 to thinking short term.

The smaller survey of HR heads matched the consultants' feedback almost perfectly. Out of a total of 15 responses, not doing enough research was mentioned five times; leaving for money and going "from" rather than "to," three times each; overestimating yourself, twice; and thinking short term, once.

First, they often don't do their homework on the job-market realities for their industry or function. Since they're not fully informed, they have unrealistic expectations when it comes to the search.

Second, they don't pay enough attention to a potential employer's financial stability and market position. Executives who would scrutinize the balance sheet of any firm they might acquire nevertheless assume that companies offering them a job must be on solid ground. Yet plenty of businesses will hire for senior jobs even when they know there's trouble ahead, so it's up to the applicant to assess how likely it is that the new job will still exist in six months.

Third, executives fail to consider cultural fit. Although hiring managers are supposed to attend to that, they often don't—and it's the new hire who will suffer most if the fit is a poor one.

Fourth, recruits assume that the official job title and description accurately reflect the role. But companies have been known to sweeten a title to attract top talent. Additionally, in a badly managed organization, people may find themselves in ill-defined jobs that have little relationship to their formal titles. One executive described his worst career move as leaving one company for a much smaller firm, where he was given the CFO title even though the bulk of his duties were really those of a COO. He found it hard to establish the credibility he needed to get the job done, given the misalignment of his tasks and title. Job candidates frequently fail to press potential employers for such specifics, including how their performance will be measured. Without that information, the success of any move depends on the luck of the draw.

Mistake 2: Leaving for money
It's easy to fall for a financially attractive offer. Search consultants told us that executives contemplating a job change rank income fourth or fifth in terms of importance but bump it to first place when making their decision. Our executive interviewees occasionally owned up to this error. Here's how the vice president of talent and engagement at an international casino company characterized his own move based on pay: "I was doing the identical role for $10K more, but leaving behind the relationships and connections was just not worth it in hindsight." Excessive focus on money is a frequently cited reason for inadequate research. "Opportunity for advancement and more money overrides the need to pursue core information," said one search consultant.

Mistake 3: Going "from" rather than "to"
Often, job seekers have become so unhappy with their present positions that they are desperate to get out. Instead of planning their career moves, they lurch from one place to the next, applying artificial urgency to the job hunt rather than waiting for the right offer. Candidates not only skimp on research in the belief that the grass has to be greener elsewhere but also fail to look strategically at their current companies for opportunities that might still exist for them.

Mistake 4: Overestimating yourself

According to one search consultant, people "believe they contribute more than they actually do and undervalue the strengths of their organization in helping them achieve their objectives." Job seekers, we found, tend to have an unrealistic view of their skills, their prospects, and occasionally their culpability. They often can't identify the sources of success and failure at their existing jobs. Candidates are "looking at the current company as being the problem and not acknowledging that they themselves may be a part of the problem," one consultant explained. Another put it this way: "People fail to be realistic sometimes [and] to be self-critical, and [they therefore think] that external circumstances and environments have more to do with their frustrations or failures than their own issues."

Their excessively optimistic view of themselves leads them to underestimate how long a job search will take and what the switching costs will be. Such job seekers also overestimate the salary they can command and their capacity to deal with the challenges of the new position—particularly the difficulty of creating change in a large organization. This last error resonated with many of the executives we interviewed. One software CFO regretted taking a job at a large multinational, where it was "so much bigger, more unwieldy, difficult to make an impact, and impersonal," he says. "No matter what I did, it didn't make a difference."

Mistake 5: Thinking short term

Having a short-term perspective can feed into each of the other four mistakes. For instance, if you overestimate yourself, you may believe you deserve rewards now, not in five years. Leaving a firm because of money and going "from" rather than "to" are both overly influenced by immediate information and considerations. "How much money can I make right now?" the executive wonders. "How can I escape an unpleasant work environment?" Still, many of the search consultants rated short-term thinking as a serious career misstep in its own right—citing it separately, not just including it as a footnote to the other mistakes.

Making Moves Under Pressure

Job seekers' mistakes aren't random. All of us feel certain psychological, social, and time pressures that can lead to any of the five we've described. Though nobody is immune, we can ask questions of ourselves and others to help ameliorate these pressures' effects.

Psychological pressure

We are all motivated to maintain a sense of psychological safety by nurturing a positive self-image, by looking at the world as a knowable and predictable place, and by avoiding risk. This can lead to an over-estimation of the self and to a habit of attending only to information that bolsters your existing beliefs. Psychologists call this selective attention "confirmation bias," and it can play havoc with a strategic job search. A hiring company presumably wants to present itself in the most flattering light, and if a candidate is motivated to move, he or she will be more than willing to see only the bright side.

Our self-protective desires go beyond the ego. We also seek to protect our material well-being by minimizing losses. Because what people give up when they leave a job is so clear (at the very worst, it's still the devil you know), excessive focus on short-term rewards and money may be a way of hedging against long-term risks that cannot really be evaluated.

Here are the fundamental questions to ask through every step of the job-change process: "What if I'm wrong? What is the evidence that this new company would be a good fit?" Do at least as much research on a company you're planning to join as you would on a company you're planning to buy stock in. Develop alternative scenarios. Consider how you'd feel about your present job if your boss left, for instance, or if the company secured an enticing new client. And rethink self-serving interpretations of events—how, for example, did your colleagues contribute to your success? This is difficult work, and it's tough to manage by yourself. Many of the executives we interviewed rely on a mentor, network, or personal "board of directors" to provide this kind of reality check.

Social pressure

Awkward social situations can trigger fight-or-flight instincts, putting strategic thinking squarely on the back burner—and they frequently lead people to make "from" rather than "to" decisions. The CFO of a marketing agency recounts such a situation from his own career, in which he changed jobs rather than have an awkward conversation or two: "Even though I enjoyed the company and had a great relationship with the CFO, I never spoke with him about my concerns before quitting. In retrospect, I realize that the CFO could have been instrumental in advancing my career within that company. If I had stayed . . . I could see myself being very happy and secure today."

Stress management techniques like yoga and meditation can help alleviate this kind of social anxiety. So can rehearsing difficult conversations, alone or with a partner. By practicing clear communication, and by repeatedly restating your concerns, you can suppress your emotional reactions and remain rational in an actual conversation. Through candid conversations with colleagues or your boss, you might be able to redeem your current job rather than make an ill-advised change.

If you are seriously contemplating a move, don't be afraid to ask tough questions at a job interview. When an interviewer can't handle direct, relevant questions, what does that say about the corporate culture?

Social discomfort intimidates us far beyond its power to harm us; as is widely known, most people rank public speaking as a fear greater than death. Deconstructing such irrational fear can help free you from the social pressures that may lead you to make hurried, unhappy career moves.

Time pressure

A hasty job change, made with insufficient information, is inherently compromised. When under time pressure, people tend to make certain predictable mistakes. They focus on readily available details like salary and job title instead of raising deeper questions, and they set their sights on the immediate future, either discounting or misreading the long term. Many also have an egocentric bias, thinking only of what affects them directly and ignoring the larger context.

Nonetheless, a career move will always involve some time pressure. To manage it, one COO in our study says he always keeps an ear to the ground with respect to industry trends, both in the U.S. and abroad. He explains that this is a way to stay ahead of the curve when it comes to career decisions. But no matter how well informed you are, you need strategies to jar yourself out of traditional ways of thinking and to make sure you aren't heeding only the nearest, loudest, quickest source of information. With the help of your mentor or network, create a list of unknowns. Engage in counter-factual-thinking exercises: Consider whether you'd take the new job if the salary were the same as your current pay. Plot the most likely three-year trajectory at each company, working out the most optimistic and pessimistic scenarios. What decision would be right in each situation?

What if you do take the wrong job? The executives we interviewed were unanimous in their views: Cut your losses and move on. Fleeing to another bad situation is not the answer, though. We suggest making your next move strategically—and wherever you are in the search process, don't hesitate to go down another road if it becomes evident that a certain kind of change wouldn't be right.

Perhaps the best protection against career-management mistakes is self-awareness. It's a broad concept, encompassing not only an understanding of your career-relevant strengths and weaknesses but also insight into the kinds of mistakes you are prone to make. It involves knowing how to correct for those tendencies, how others perceive you, when to consult a trusted mentor or network, what elements of a job make it truly satisfying for you, and what constitutes a healthy work-life balance.

Originally published in January–February 2010. Reprint R1001M

Learning to Learn

by Erika Andersen

ORGANIZATIONS TODAY ARE IN CONSTANT FLUX. Industries are consolidating, new business models are emerging, new technologies are being developed, and consumer behaviors are evolving. For executives, the ever-increasing pace of change can be especially demanding. It forces them to understand and quickly respond to big shifts in the way companies operate and how work must get done. In the words of Arie de Geus, a business theorist, "The ability to learn faster than your competitors may be the only sustainable competitive advantage."

I'm not talking about relaxed armchair or even structured classroom learning. I'm talking about resisting the bias against doing new things, scanning the horizon for growth opportunities, and pushing yourself to acquire radically different capabilities—while still performing your job. That requires a willingness to experiment and become a novice again and again: an extremely discomforting notion for most of us.

Over decades of coaching and consulting to thousands of executives in a variety of industries, however, my colleagues and I have come across people who succeed at this kind of learning. We've identified four attributes they have in spades: aspiration, self-awareness, curiosity, and vulnerability. They truly want to understand and master new skills; they see themselves very clearly; they constantly think of and ask good questions; and they tolerate their own mistakes as they move up the learning curve.

Of course, these things come more naturally to some people than to others. But, drawing on research in psychology and management as well as our work with clients, we have identified some fairly simple mental tools anyone can develop to boost all four attributes—even those that are often considered fixed (aspiration, curiosity, and vulnerability).

Aspiration

It's easy to see aspiration as either there or not: You want to learn a new skill or you don't; you have ambition and motivation or you lack them. But great learners can raise their aspiration level—and that's key, because everyone is guilty of sometimes resisting development that is critical to success.

Think about the last time your company adopted a new approach—overhauled a reporting system, replaced a CRM platform, revamped the supply chain. Were you eager to go along? I doubt it. Your initial response was probably to justify not learning. (*It will take too long. The old way works just fine for me. I bet it's just a flash in the pan.*) When confronted with new learning, this is often our first roadblock: We focus on the negative and unconsciously reinforce our lack of aspiration.

When we *do* want to learn something, we focus on the positive—what we'll gain from learning it—and envision a happy future in which we're reaping those rewards. That propels us into action. Researchers have found that shifting your focus from challenges to benefits is a good way to increase your aspiration to do initially unappealing things. For example, when Nicole Detling, a psychologist at the University of Utah, encouraged aerialists and speed skaters to picture themselves benefiting from a particular skill, they were much more motivated to practice it.

A few years ago I coached a CMO who was hesitant to learn about big data. Even though most of his peers were becoming converts, he'd convinced himself that he didn't have the time to get into it and that it wouldn't be that important to his industry. I finally realized

Idea in Brief

The ever-increasing pace of change in today's organizations requires that executives understand and then quickly respond to constant shifts in how their businesses operate and how work must get done. That means you must resist your innate biases against doing new things in new ways, scan the horizon for growth opportunities, and push yourself to acquire drastically different capabilities—while still doing your existing job. To succeed, you must be willing to experiment and become a novice over and over again, which for most of us is an extremely discomforting proposition.

Over decades of work with managers, the author has found that people who do succeed at this kind of learning have four well-developed attributes: aspiration, self-awareness, curiosity, and vulnerability. They have a deep desire to understand and master new skills; they see themselves very clearly; they're constantly thinking of and asking good questions; and they tolerate their own mistakes as they move up the curve. Andersen has identified some fairly simple mental strategies that anyone can use to boost these attributes.

that this was an aspiration problem and encouraged him to think of ways that getting up to speed on data-driven marketing could help him personally. He acknowledged that it would be useful to know more about how various segments of his customer base were responding to his team's online advertising and in-store marketing campaigns. I then invited him to imagine the situation he'd be in a year later if he was getting that data. He started to show some excitement, saying, "We would be testing different approaches simultaneously, both in-store and online; we'd have good, solid information about which ones were working and for whom; and we could save a lot of time and money by jettisoning the less effective approaches faster." I could almost feel his aspiration rising. Within a few months he'd hired a data analytics expert, made a point of learning from her on a daily basis, and begun to rethink key campaigns in light of his new perspective and skills.

Self-Awareness

Over the past decade or so, most leaders have grown familiar with the concept of self-awareness. They understand that they need to solicit feedback and recognize how others see them. But when it comes to the need for learning, our assessments of ourselves—what we know and don't know, skills we have and don't have—can still be woefully inaccurate. In one study conducted by David Dunning, a Cornell University psychologist, 94% of college professors reported that they were doing "above average work." Clearly, almost half were wrong—many extremely so—and their self-deception surely diminished any appetite for development. Only 6% of respondents saw themselves as having a lot to learn about being an effective teacher.

In my work I've found that the people who evaluate themselves most accurately start the process inside their own heads: They accept that their perspective is often biased or flawed and then strive for greater objectivity, which leaves them much more open to hearing and acting on others' opinions. The trick is to pay attention to how you talk to yourself about yourself and then question the validity of that "self-talk."

Let's say your boss has told you that your team isn't strong enough and that you need to get better at assessing and developing talent. Your initial reaction might be something like *What? She's wrong. My team is strong.* Most of us respond defensively to that sort of criticism. But as soon as you recognize what you're thinking, ask yourself, *Is that accurate? What facts do I have to support it?* In the process of reflection you may discover that you're wrong and your boss is right, or that the truth lies somewhere in between—you cover for some of your reports by doing things yourself, and one of them is inconsistent in meeting deadlines; however, two others are stars. Your inner voice is most useful when it reports the facts of a situation in this balanced way. It should serve as a "fair witness" so that you're open to seeing the areas in which you could improve and how to do so.

One CEO I know was convinced that he was a great manager and leader. He did have tremendous industry knowledge and great

Changing your inner narrative

Unsupportive self-talk	Supportive self-talk
I don't need to learn this.	What would my future look like if I did?
I'm already fine at this.	Am I really? How do I compare with my peers?
This is boring.	I wonder why others find it interesting.
I'm terrible at this.	I'm making beginner mistakes, but I'll get better.

instincts about growing his business, and his board acknowledged those strengths. But he listened only to people who affirmed his view of himself and dismissed input about shortcomings; his team didn't feel engaged or inspired. When he finally started to question his assumptions (*Is everyone on my team focused and productive? If not, is there something I could be doing differently?*), he became much more aware of his developmental needs and open to feedback. He realized that it wasn't enough to have strategic insights; he had to share them with his reports and invite discussion, and then set clear priorities—backed by quarterly team and individual goals, regular progress checks, and troubleshooting sessions.

Curiosity

Kids are relentless in their urge to learn and master. As John Medina writes in *Brain Rules,* "This need for explanation is so powerfully stitched into their experience that some scientists describe it as a drive, just as hunger and thirst and sex are drives." Curiosity is what makes us try something until we can do it, or think about something until we understand it. Great learners retain this childhood drive, or regain it through another application of self-talk. Instead of focusing on and reinforcing initial disinterest in a new subject, they learn to ask themselves "curious questions" about it and follow those questions up with actions. Carol Sansone, a psychology researcher, has found, for example, that people can increase their willingness to tackle necessary tasks by thinking about how they could do the work differently to make it more interesting. In other words, they change their self-talk from *This is boring* to *I wonder if I could . . . ?*

You can employ the same strategy in your working life by noticing the language you use in thinking about things that already interest you—*How . . . ? Why . . . ? I wonder . . . ?*—and drawing on it when you need to become curious. Then take just one step to answer a question you've asked yourself: Read an article, query an expert, find a teacher, join a group—whatever feels easiest.

I recently worked with a corporate lawyer whose firm had offered her a bigger job that required knowledge of employment law—an area she regarded as "the single most boring aspect of the legal profession." Rather than trying to persuade her otherwise, I asked her what she was curious about and why. "Swing dancing," she said. "I'm fascinated by the history of it. I wonder how it developed, and whether it was a response to the Depression—it's such a happy art form. I watch great dancers and think about why they do certain things."

I explained that her "curious language" could be applied to employment law. "I wonder how anyone could find it interesting?" she said jokingly. I told her that was actually an OK place to start. She began thinking out loud about possible answers ("Maybe some lawyers see it as a way to protect both their employees and their companies . . .") and then proposed a few other curious questions ("How might knowing more about this make me a better lawyer?").

Soon she was intrigued enough to connect with a colleague who was experienced in employment law. She asked him what he found interesting about it and how he had acquired his knowledge, and his answers prompted other questions. Over the following months she learned what she needed to know for that aspect of her new role.

The next time you're asked to learn something at the office, or sense that you should because colleagues are doing so, encourage yourself to ask and answer a few curious questions about it—*Why are others so excited about this? How might this make my job easier?*—and then seek out the answers. You'll need to find just one thing about a "boring" topic that sparks your curiosity.

Vulnerability

Once we become good or even excellent at some things, we rarely want to go back to being *not* good at other things. Yes, we're now taught to embrace experimentation and "fast failure" at work. But we're also taught to play to our strengths. So the idea of being bad at something for weeks or months; feeling awkward and slow; having to ask "dumb," "I-don't-know-what-you're-talking-about" questions; and needing step-by-step guidance again and again is extremely scary. Great learners allow themselves to be vulnerable enough to accept that beginner state. In fact, they become reasonably comfortable in it—by managing their self-talk.

Generally, when we're trying something new and doing badly at it, we think terrible thoughts: *I hate this. I'm such an idiot. I'll never get this right. This is so frustrating!* That static in our brains leaves little bandwidth for learning. The ideal mindset for a beginner is both vulnerable and balanced: *I'm going to be bad at this to start with, because I've never done it before. AND I know I can learn to do it over time.* In fact, the researchers Robert Wood and Albert Bandura found in the late 1980s that when people are encouraged to expect mistakes and learn from them early in the process of acquiring new skills, the result is "heightened interest, persistence, and better performance."

I know a senior sales manager from the United States who was recently tapped to run the Asia-Pacific region for his company. He was having a hard time acclimating to living overseas and working with colleagues from other cultures, and he responded by leaning on his sales expertise rather than acknowledging his beginner status in the new environment. I helped him recognize his resistance to being a cultural novice, and he was able to shift his self-talk from *This is so uncomfortable—I'll just focus on what I already know* to *I have a lot to learn about Asian cultures. I'm a quick study, so I'll be able to pick it up.* He told me it was an immediate relief: Simply acknowledging his novice status made him feel less foolish and more relaxed. He started asking the necessary questions, and soon he was seen as open, interested, and beginning to understand his new environment.

The ability to acquire new skills and knowledge quickly and continually is crucial to success in a world of rapid change. If you don't currently have the aspiration, self-awareness, curiosity, and vulnerability to be an effective learner, these simple tools can help you get there.

Originally published in March 2016. Reprint R1603J

The Strategic Side Gig

by Ken Banta and Orlan Boston

AMIT PALEY SPENT the first seven years of his career as a reporter for the *Washington Post*. While he put in long hours and did stints in war zones in the Middle East, he also made time to serve on the board of his alma mater's newspaper, where he could help aspiring journalists and learn how nonprofits worked. After leaving the *Post* and attending business school, Paley joined McKinsey as a consultant—another demanding job. But again, he made it a priority to volunteer, this time staffing nighttime and weekend phone lines for the Trevor Project, an organization that works to prevent suicides among LGBTQ youth. Eventually he joined its board (full disclosure: one of us also serves on it), which gave him exposure to the operational and financial challenges of such groups and inspired him to get more involved in McKinsey's nonprofit work. This virtuous cycle eventually culminated in his being named CEO of the Trevor Project in 2017. "By investing my time outside work in things I was passionate about, I learned things that made me better at my job," Paley explains. "Those experiences also prepared me for future leadership roles that I didn't know I would have."

That's the power of strategically taking on *extra* jobs *outside* your organization.

What Is External Engagement?

A lot of managers and leaders focus obsessively on their current jobs and companies. Many believe they simply can't be successful without that kind of single-mindedness. Of course, most people now realize that to advance in your career, especially to the C-suite, you need diverse experiences and should explore opportunities in a variety of functions, industries, and geographies. But the general thinking is that when you get a challenging stretch role, you should give it all your attention to make sure you excel and position yourself for the next step. That approach can pay off in the short term. However, in our combined work with thousands of executives as well as in our own experience, we've found that it can stymie your long-term development—and even your career.

Why? Now more than ever, engagement in strategic side gigs is a requirement for executives. The pace of change and disruption is also making it difficult for corporate learning departments, management schools, and executive education programs to keep their curricula relevant. As a result, leaders who want to rise—and help their organizations thrive—need to find ways to expand their field of vision and build their knowledge, skills, and connections even as they carry on their daily work.

This goes well beyond attending industry conferences and networking events or taking classes at night. We're talking about meaningful engagement in outside activities that expose you to different people, information, and cultures but are also in some way synergistic with both your personal interests and your current or future primary work. That can include membership on public, private, or nonprofit boards; teaching, fellowships, publishing, or film production; public or civic service at the federal, state, or municipal level; advising or investing in start-ups; leadership roles in professional associations and clubs; and speaking at or organizing idea forums, festivals, and conferences. Think of yourself as having a portfolio where your job is squarely in the middle, various outside activities surround and complement it, and you deploy what you've learned in each realm to the others.

Idea in Brief

If you have a big job, the thinking goes, you should focus on it obsessively so that you excel and position yourself for the next role. But, in fact, such single-mindedness can stymie your career. Leaders need to find ways to expand their range of knowledge, skills, and connections outside their daily work. This goes beyond attending conferences or even taking classes; it requires meaningful engagement in outside activities, such as work on boards, in teaching or public service, in mentoring start-ups, and in leadership roles for associations and clubs. This article explains how to find time in your hectic schedule, identify the side gigs that will be synergistic with your personal interests and current job, and get your employer's buy-in. Taking on extracurricular activities isn't always easy, but in the end it can open opportunities up for you and become your personal competitive advantage.

When we surveyed 122 senior executives from a spectrum of industries, all agreed that outside engagements were critical to leadership success today and going forward. All but one said that organizations also benefit when employees have such experiences. More than 100 told us that they have even considered people's external activities when assessing their fit in succession planning.

To learn how leaders find the right opportunities and what they gain from them, we conducted in-depth interviews with private- and public-sector leaders of varying ages and career stages who exemplified that philosophy. In this article we've distilled their lessons.

How Can You Make It Happen?

Finding the time

One of the biggest constraints executives face is an already packed schedule. Given all your professional and personal demands, it might seem impossible to add anything to your plate. But it's been our shared experience that you can find the time if you make it a priority (though it may mean giving up some nights and weekends). You can, for instance, block off one or more hours a week on your calendar for these activities. Inviting your friends, spouse, or family members—people you want to spend time with anyway—to join you in them can be an enriching win-win. If you can also involve a small group of like-minded professionals or perhaps younger staff who share your interests, it will help keep you committed and give you people with whom to compare notes. And if you get buy-in from your boss, he or she might allow you to devote office hours to your outside passion.

How much time should you spend on these "extracurricular" activities? Our survey respondents said 10% to 20%, but the amount needn't be consistent every day, week, or month. Often you can space out your commitments to external projects. The balance can and should shift to as low as 2% when your work and home lives are extremely busy, or as high as 30% when they're not. In other words, you need to deliver in your job and for your family before you can take on additional responsibilities. But if things lighten up, seize the opportunity.

Kara Medoff Barnett is the executive director of the American Ballet Theatre and the mother of three girls, ages 10, eight, and four. But she's also involved in the American Theater Wing, which keeps her connected to a different kind of performance art, and she just completed a five-year stint as a term member on the Council on Foreign Relations, which helps her better understand the issues facing her organization's dancers, who come from some 15 countries. "I put a lot of thought into what I can and can't handle outside my full-time day job and active family life," she explains. That includes saying not just "no" but also "not now" to many groups and being very deliberate about her schedule by, for example, always reserving Friday nights for time with her husband and kids. "The key is being present in the room you are in," she says. "When you're in work mode, be all-in. When you're home with your kids, put your phone away so that you can read bedtime stories without checking email. And as for the other activities, participate in the ones that spark your intellectual curiosity. Meet people you wouldn't encounter in your current industry or workplace. Open your aperture."

The late David Stern, a lawyer who became the commissioner of the National Basketball Association, served on various boards throughout his career and agreed that it was important to fit those meaningful outside commitments into an already hectic schedule. He noted that his own early exposure to different people and problem-solving approaches equipped him to negotiate a groundbreaking collective bargaining agreement between the NBA's players and owners in 2011. "No matter how busy you are, you should be learning," he explained to us. "That was something I always pushed myself on by asking: 'What did I do to stretch myself today?' I think there is a lot to be learned outside the office."

Identifying roles

How can you find the right opportunities—ones that create the kind of virtuous cycle we described earlier? First, spread the word within your organization and to your trusted contacts that you're looking for outside activities relevant to your job or the skills needed in it. Explore your passions and see if groups connected to them have any open positions that would give you a chance to learn and develop. Seek out friends and colleagues who already have meaningful volunteer jobs and offer to help them. Get your name, interests, and expertise out there through public speaking, social media, and publishing so that people start presenting possibilities to you.

"Take baby steps," advises Mehmood Khan, the former chief scientific officer of global research and development at PepsiCo and now the CEO of Life Biosciences. Khan has served on multiple advisory boards, including one that allowed him, when in his thirties, to help craft public health policy. "You can do a lot on your own time, such as helping nonprofits in the community where you live," he says. "Look for these opportunities. Every experience can be a value-add."

After this period of exploration and experimentation, you'll want to be highly selective about the roles you commit to seriously. "It's incredibly important when you engage in activities outside work that you do it for sincere reasons and not just as a way to self-promote or to rub shoulders with potential professional connections," says Kathryn Wylde, the president and CEO of the Partnership for New York City, which runs the David Rockefeller Fellows Program (in which Orlan participated).

Paley agrees: "If you're spending your free time on something that you're not passionate about or that doesn't give you energy, it's a missed opportunity both for you and for anyone who might otherwise benefit from your insights."

Ensure, too, that you're picking a role in which you can really make a worthwhile contribution. Ken Mehlman, who was formerly in politics but is now the global head of public affairs and cohead of global impact at the investment firm KKR, currently holds board positions at Mount Sinai Hospital of New York, Franklin & Marshall College, Teach for America, and Sponsors for Educational Opportunity. He notes, "I have always tried to find institutions to get involved in where I can make a measurable difference."

Justifying your commitment

When you take on a strategic side gig, it's often wise to ask for permission (or sometimes forgiveness) from your employer and family. The key is to show the relevance, including both personal benefits, such as increased engagement and energy, and organizational ones, such as a broader network. (More on this below.) "Challenge your organization in an appropriate manner," advises Khan. "Have a clear story about how the activity benefits your company and your development, and its alignment with company values. Make a case for why it's synergistic."

You can even talk to your boss about making external engagements one of your annual objectives or aligning your outside passion with the interests of your employer. For example, in Orlan's roles as an EY executive and a board member for the Trevor Project, he helped create a formal strategic relationship between the two, which allowed the nonprofit to tap into EY resources and staff.

Earlier in Medoff Barnett's career, when she was the managing director of Lincoln Center International and her girls were even younger than they are now, she was selected for an Aspen Institute fellowship that required her to spend four weeks away from home over a two-year period. Despite being a young mother with a huge job, she knew it would be "a transformational personal and professional growth experience," so she negotiated with her bosses, employees, and husband—what she describes as "an incredible team back at home"—to make it happen.

If your employer balks at letting you devote time to an outside cause even after you've made the case that it will add value to you and the company, that's a red flag. As Khan says, "If the organization you work for doesn't understand the value in engaging on the outside, it's at risk of becoming obsolete. Why would you want to be part of that?"

What Are the Long-Term Benefits?

Recharging your energy

Keith Krach, a serial entrepreneur, a cofounder of Ariba, and the former CEO and chairman of DocuSign, who was recently appointed U.S. undersecretary of state for economic growth, energy, and the environment, says that when you squeeze in time for outside activities, it can actually help you avoid burnout. "I've found that the busier you are, the more you can take on, and you definitely get better at your job," he says. During his career, which began in General Motors' engineering group, he has served on various nonprofit and corporate boards (including those of Angie's List and Opportunity International) and helped create a leadership-training program for Purdue University's Sigma Chi fraternity, for which he still serves as a mentor. "Every time I take a week to go facilitate the program for these kids, my batteries are recharged," he says. "I get inspired. It makes me think thoughts I never would have had otherwise. It broadens my scope of empathy and understanding. As my mom always told me, the best way to learn is through OPE: other people's experiences."

Building knowledge, skills, and confidence

The best external engagement gives you something to bring back to your own organization. A great example comes from Rosanne Haggerty, the president and CEO of Community Solutions, an organization dedicated to ending homelessness and its causes. At age 30 she started her first nonprofit and, about that same time, applied to be on

How Organizations Can Inspire Outside Engagement

INCREASINGLY, OPPORTUNITIES TO ENGAGE in meaningful work outside the office are becoming an employee recruitment and retention tool. Millennials and members of Generation Z in particular want to know that their employers value their personal development and the contributions they make not just to their companies but also to their communities.

Case in point: KKR's head of public affairs, Ken Mehlman, says that his firm has implemented a program called 40 for 40, which gives employees 40 hours of paid time each year to serve at nonprofits they feel passionate about. In the four years since it was launched, some 1,000 KKR employees have spent nearly 11,000 hours working for 220 charitable organizations. "There are so many opportunities for an organization to benefit when you build relationships with people outside work," says Mehlman. "You learn to think about problems in one context and apply them in another."

---

the board of trustees of her alma mater, Amherst College. Although it was daunting to take on the two commitments at once, she says, "the timing was perfect in that I received a remarkable education about what it meant to work with a board and what to pay attention to as I grew my own nonprofit. Serving on that board was like taking a master class in nonprofit leadership and long-term stewardship. Wherever you are on your career journey, anytime you can learn new skills, manage a complex project, and even make some mistakes you can bounce back from, it will be extremely valuable."

Developing a broader perspective

When you do important work in other fields and join other networks, you uncover areas of untapped opportunity for yourself and your organization. You can make connections that help you become a better innovator and manager. Ten years into her first nonprofit CEO role, Haggerty took time off to go to Tokyo on a fellowship and study the Japanese prefabricated housing industry and how a different society was responding to homelessness. "It redirected my thinking in ways that still reverberate," she says.

David Pyott, the former chairman and CEO of Allergan, served on multiple boards outside the pharmaceutical industry during his career and encouraged his subordinates to do the same. "You realize how different the world looks from the other side," he explains. He says the extra roles he took on helped him meet more potential commercial partners, better identify trends, and understand prospective markets for products such as Botox.

All this adds up to a more well-rounded leadership mindset. As Mehlman notes, "Lateral thinking beats linear thinking every day of the week. What's critical these days is to bring a different perspective and apply it to whatever you're doing. And you can't do that if all your attention and focus is limited to the four walls of your organization."

Finding the right engagement outside your day job isn't always easy. But once you do it, it usually opens the door to many other opportunities. And it's those experiences that will become your personal competitive advantage. "As the business world becomes more complex, it's increasingly difficult to find solutions in a single field or discipline," Khan concludes. "To develop as a leader, you need to leave your comfort zone. That's how personal growth occurs."

Originally published in May–June 2020. Reprint R2003L

How Leaders Create and Use Networks

by Herminia Ibarra and Mark Lee Hunter

WHEN HENRIK BALMER BECAME the production manager and a board member of a newly bought-out cosmetics firm, improving his network was the last thing on his mind. The main problem he faced was time: Where would he find the hours to guide his team through a major upgrade of the production process and then think about strategic issues like expanding the business? The only way he could carve out time and still get home to his family at a decent hour was to lock himself—literally—in his office. Meanwhile, there were day-to-day issues to resolve, like a recurring conflict with his sales director over custom orders that compromised production efficiency. Networking, which Henrik defined as the unpleasant task of trading favors with strangers, was a luxury he could not afford. But when a new acquisition was presented at a board meeting without his input, he abruptly realized he was out of the loop—not just inside the company, but outside, too—at a moment when his future in the company was at stake.

Henrik's case is not unusual. Over the past two years, we have been following a cohort of 30 managers making their way through what we call the leadership transition, an inflection point in their careers that challenges them to rethink both themselves and their roles. In the process, we've found that networking—creating a fabric of personal contacts who will provide support, feedback, insight, resources, and information—is simultaneously one of the most self-evident and one of the most dreaded developmental challenges that aspiring leaders must address.

Their discomfort is understandable. Typically, managers rise through the ranks by dint of a strong command of the technical elements of their jobs and a nose-to-the-grindstone focus on accomplishing their teams' objectives. When challenged to move beyond their functional specialties and address strategic issues facing the overall business, many managers do not immediately grasp that this will involve relational—not analytical—tasks. Nor do they easily understand that exchanges and interactions with a diverse array of current and potential stakeholders are not distractions from their "real work" but are actually at the heart of their new leadership roles.

Like Henrik (whose identity we've disguised, along with all the other managers we describe here), a majority of the managers we work with say that they find networking insincere or manipulative—at best, an elegant way of using people. Not surprisingly, for every manager who instinctively constructs and maintains a useful network, we see several who struggle to overcome this innate resistance. Yet the alternative to networking is to fail—either in reaching for a leadership position or in succeeding at it.

Watching our emerging leaders approach this daunting task, we discovered that three distinct but interdependent forms of networking—*operational, personal*, and *strategic*—played a vital role in their transitions. The first helped them manage current internal responsibilities, the second boosted their personal development, and the third opened their eyes to new business directions and the stakeholders they would need to enlist. While our managers differed in how well they pursued operational and personal networking, we discovered that almost all of them underutilized strategic networking. In this article, we describe key features of each networking form (summarized in the table "The three forms of networking") and, using our managers' experiences, explain how a three-pronged networking strategy can become part and parcel of a new leader's development plan.

Idea in Brief

What separates successful leaders from the rest of the pack? Networking: creating a tissue of personal contacts to provide the support, feedback, and resources needed to get things done.

Yet many leaders avoid networking. Some think they don't have time for it. Others disdain it as manipulative.

To succeed as a leader, Ibarra and Hunter recommend building three types of networks:

- **Operational**—people you need to accomplish your assigned, routine tasks.

- **Personal**—kindred spirits outside your organization who can help you with personal advancement.

- **Strategic**—people outside your control who will enable you to reach key organizational objectives.

You need all three types of networks. But to *really* succeed, you must master strategic networking—by interacting regularly with people who can open your eyes to new business opportunities and help you capitalize on them. Build your strategic network, and burnish your own—and your company's—performance.

Operational Networking

All managers need to build good working relationships with the people who can help them do their jobs. The number and breadth of people involved can be impressive—such operational networks include not only direct reports and superiors but also peers within an operational unit, other internal players with the power to block or support a project, and key outsiders such as suppliers, distributors, and customers. The purpose of this type of networking is to ensure coordination and cooperation among people who have to know and trust one another in order to accomplish their immediate tasks. That isn't always easy, but it is relatively straightforward, because the task provides focus and a clear criterion for membership in the network: Either you're necessary to the job and helping to get it done, or you're not.

Although operational networking was the form that came most naturally to the managers we studied, nearly every one had

Idea in Practice

The most effective leaders understand the differences among the three types of networks and how to build them.

	Operational network	Personal network	Strategic network
Network's purpose	Get work done efficiently.	Develop professional skills through coaching and mentoring; exchange important referrals and needed outside information.	Figure out future priorities and challenges; get stakeholder support for them.
How to find network members	Identify individuals who can block or support a project.	Participate in professional associations, alumni groups, clubs, and personal-interest communities.	Identify lateral and vertical relationships with other functional and business-unit managers—people outside your immediate control—who can help you determine how your role and contribution fit into the overall picture.

important blind spots regarding people and groups they depended on to make things happen. In one case, Alistair, an accounting manager who worked in an entrepreneurial firm with several hundred employees, was suddenly promoted by the company's founder to financial director and given a seat on the board. He was both the youngest and the least-experienced board member, and his instinctive response to these new responsibilities was to reestablish his functional credentials. Acting on a hint from the founder that the company might go public, Alistair undertook a reorganization of the accounting department that would enable the books to withstand close scrutiny. Alistair succeeded brilliantly in upgrading his team's capabilities, but he missed the fact that only a minority of the seven-person board shared the founder's ambition. A year

Leveraging Your Networks

Networking takes work. To lessen the pain and increase the gain:

- **Mind your mind-set.** Accept that networking is one of the most important requirements of a leadership role. To overcome any qualms about it, identify a person you respect who networks effectively and ethically. Observe how he or she uses networks to accomplish goals.

- **Reallocate your time.** Master the art of delegation, to liberate time you can then spend on cultivating networks.

- **Establish connections.** Create reasons for interacting with people outside your function or organization; for instance, by taking advantage of social interests to set the stage for addressing strategic concerns.

  Example: An investment banker invited key clients to the theatre (a passion of hers) several times a year. Through these events, she developed her own business *and* learned things about her clients' companies that generated business and ideas for other divisions in her firm.

- **Give and take continually.** Don't wait until you really need something badly to ask for a favor from a network member. Instead, take every opportunity to give to—and receive from—people in your networks, whether you need help or not.

into Alistair's tenure, discussion about whether to take the company public polarized the board, and he discovered that all that time cleaning up the books might have been better spent sounding out his codirectors.

One of the problems with an exclusive reliance on operational networks is that they are usually geared toward meeting objectives as assigned, not toward asking the strategic question, "What *should* we be doing?" By the same token, managers do not exercise as much personal choice in assembling operational relationships as they do in weaving personal and strategic networks, because to a large extent the right relationships are prescribed by the job and organizational structure. Thus, most operational networking occurs within an organization, and ties are determined in large part by routine, short-term demands. Relationships formed with outsiders, such as board members, customers, and regulators, are directly task-related and tend to be bounded and constrained by demands determined at a higher level. Of course, an individual manager can choose to deepen and develop the ties to different extents, and all managers exercise discretion over who gets priority attention. It's the quality of relationships—the rapport and mutual trust—that gives an operational network its power. Nonetheless, the substantial constraints on network membership mean these connections are unlikely to deliver value to managers beyond assistance with the task at hand.

The typical manager in our group was more concerned with sustaining cooperation within the existing network than with building relationships to face nonroutine or unforeseen challenges. But as a manager moves into a leadership role, his or her network must reorient itself externally and toward the future.

Personal Networking

We observed that once aspiring leaders like Alistair awaken to the dangers of an excessively internal focus, they begin to seek kindred spirits outside their organizations. Simultaneously, they become aware of the limitations of their social skills, such as a lack of knowledge about professional domains beyond their own, which makes it difficult for them to find common ground with people outside their usual circles. Through professional associations, alumni groups, clubs, and personal interest communities, managers gain new perspectives that allow them to advance in their careers. This is what we mean by personal networking.

Many of the managers we study question why they should spend precious time on an activity so indirectly related to the work at hand. Why widen one's circle of casual acquaintances when there isn't time even for urgent tasks? The answer is that these contacts provide important referrals, information, and, often, developmental support such as coaching and mentoring. A newly appointed factory director, for example, faced with a turnaround-or-close-down situation that was paralyzing his staff, joined a business organization—and through it met a lawyer who became his counsel in the turnaround. Buoyed by his success, he networked within his company's headquarters in search of someone who had dealt with a similar crisis. Eventually, he found two mentors.

A personal network can also be a safe space for personal development and as such can provide a foundation for strategic networking. The experience of Timothy, a principal in a midsize software company, is a good example. Like his father, Timothy stuttered. When he had the opportunity to prepare for meetings, his stutter was not an issue, but spontaneous encounters inside and outside the company were dreadfully painful. To solve this problem, he began accepting at least two invitations per week to the social gatherings he had assiduously ignored before. Before each event, he asked who else had been invited and did background research on the other guests so that he could initiate conversations. The hardest part, he said, was "getting through the door." Once inside, his interest in the conversations helped him forget himself and master his stutter. As his stutter diminished, he also applied himself to networking across his company, whereas previously he had taken refuge in his technical expertise. Like Timothy, several of our emerging leaders successfully used personal networking as a relatively safe way to expose problems and seek insight into solutions—safe, that is, compared with strategic networking, in which the stakes are far higher.

Personal networks are largely external, made up of discretionary links to people with whom we have something in common. As a result, what makes a personal network powerful is its referral potential. According to the famous six degrees of separation principle, our personal contacts are valuable to the extent that they help us reach, in as few connections as possible, the far-off person who has the information we need.

In watching managers struggle to widen their professional relationships in ways that feel both natural and legitimate to them, we repeatedly saw them shift their time and energy from operational to personal networking. For people who have rarely looked outside their organizations, this is an important first step, one that fosters a

The three forms of networking

Managers who think they are adept at networking are often operating only at an operational or personal level.
Effective leaders learn to employ networks for strategic purposes.

	Operational	Personal	Strategic
Purpose	Getting work done efficiently; maintaining the capacities and functions required of the group.	Enhancing personal and professional development; providing referrals to useful information and contacts.	Figuring out future priorities and challenges; getting stakeholder support for them.
Location and temporal orientation	Contacts are mostly internal and oriented toward current demands.	Contacts are mostly external and oriented toward current interests and future potential interests.	Contacts are internal and external and oriented toward the future.
Players and recruitment	Key contacts are relatively non-discretionary; they are prescribed mostly by the task and organizational structure, so it is very clear who is relevant.	Key contacts are mostly discretionary; it is not always clear who is relevant.	Key contacts follow from the strategic context and the organizational environment, but specific membership is discretionary; it is not always clear who is relevant.
Network attributes and key behaviors	Depth: building strong working relationships.	Breadth: reaching out to contacts who can make referrals.	Leverage: creating inside-outside links.

deeper understanding of themselves and the environments in which they move. Ultimately, however, personal networking alone won't propel managers through the leadership transition. Aspiring leaders may find people who awaken new interests but fail to become comfortable with the power players at the level above them. Or they may achieve new influence within a professional community but fail to harness those ties in the service of organizational goals. That's why managers who know they need to develop their networking skills, and make a real effort to do so, nonetheless may end up feeling like they have wasted their time and energy. As we'll see, personal networking will not help a manager through the leadership transition unless he or she learns how to bring those connections to bear on organizational strategy.

Strategic Networking

When managers begin the delicate transition from functional manager to business leader, they must start to concern themselves with broad strategic issues. Lateral and vertical relationships with other functional and business unit managers—all people outside their immediate control—become a lifeline for figuring out how their own contributions fit into the big picture. Thus strategic networking plugs the aspiring leader into a set of relationships and information sources that collectively embody the power to achieve personal and organizational goals.

Operating beside players with diverse affiliations, backgrounds, objectives, and incentives requires a manager to formulate business rather than functional objectives, and to work through the coalitions and networks needed to sell ideas and compete for resources. Consider Sophie, a manager who, after rising steadily through the ranks in logistics and distribution, was stupefied to learn that the CEO was considering a radical reorganization of her function that would strip her of some responsibilities. Rewarded to date for incremental annual improvements, she had failed to notice shifting priorities in the wider market and the resulting internal shuffle for resources and power at the higher levels of her company. Although she had

From Functional Manager to Business Leader: How Companies Can Help

EXECUTIVES WHO OVERSEE MANAGEMENT development know how to spot critical inflection points: the moments when highly successful people must change their perspective on what is important and, accordingly, how they spend their time. Many organizations still promote people on the basis of their performance in roles whose requirements differ dramatically from those of leadership roles. And many new leaders feel that they are going it alone, without coaching or guidance. By being sensitive to the fact that most strong technical or functional managers lack the capabilities required to build strategic networks that advance their personal and professional goals, human resources and learning professionals can take steps to help in this important area.

For example, Genesis Park, an innovative in-house leadership development program at PricewaterhouseCoopers, focuses explicitly on building networks. The five-month program, during which participants are released from their client responsibilities, includes business case development, strategic projects, team building, change management projects, and in-depth discussions with business leaders from inside and outside the company. The young leaders who participate end up with a strong internal-external nexus of ties to support them as their careers evolve.

---

built a loyal, high-performing team, she had few relationships outside her group to help her anticipate the new imperatives, let alone give her ideas about how to respond. After she argued that distribution issues were her purview, and failed to be persuasive, she hired consultants to help her prepare a counterproposal. But Sophie's boss simply concluded that she lacked a broad, longer-term business perspective. Frustrated, Sophie contemplated leaving the company. Only after some patient coaching from a senior manager did she understand that she had to get out of her unit and start talking to opinion leaders inside and outside the company to form a sellable plan for the future.

What differentiates a leader from a manager, research tells us, is the ability to figure out where to go and to enlist the people and groups necessary to get there. Recruiting stakeholders, lining up allies and sympathizers, diagnosing the political landscape, and brokering conversations among unconnected parties are all part of

Companies that recognize the importance of leadership networking can also do a lot to help people overcome their innate discomfort by creating natural ways for them to extend their networks. When Nissan CEO Carlos Ghosn sought to break down crippling internal barriers at the company, he created cross-functional teams of middle managers from diverse units and charged them with proposing solutions to problems ranging from supply costs to product design. Nissan subsequently institutionalized the teams, not just as a way to solve problems but also to encourage lateral networks. Rather than avoid the extra work, aspiring leaders ask for these assignments.

Most professional development is based on the notion that successful people acquire new role-appropriate skills as they move up the hierarchy. But making the transition from manager to leader requires subtraction as well as addition: To make room for new competencies, managers must rely less on their older, well-honed skills. To do so, they must change their perspective on how to add value and what to contribute. Eventually, they must also transform how they think and who they are. Companies that help their top talent reinvent themselves will better prepare them for a successful leadership transition.

a leader's job. As they step up to the leadership transition, some managers accept their growing dependence on others and seek to transform it into mutual influence. Others dismiss such work as "political" and, as a result, undermine their ability to advance their goals.

Several of the participants in our sample chose the latter approach, justifying their choice as a matter of personal values and integrity. In one case, Jody, who managed a department in a large company under what she described as "dysfunctional" leadership, refused even to try to activate her extensive network within the firm when internal adversaries took over key functions of her unit. When we asked her why she didn't seek help from anyone in the organization to stop this coup, she replied that she refused to play "stupid political games. . . . You can only do what you think is the ethical and right thing from your perspective." Stupid or not, those games cost her the respect and support of her direct reports and coworkers, who hesitated to follow someone they perceived as unwilling to defend herself. Eventually she had no choice but to leave.

The key to a good strategic network is leverage: the ability to marshal information, support, and resources from one sector of a network to achieve results in another. Strategic networkers use indirect influence, convincing one person in the network to get someone else, who is not in the network, to take a needed action. Moreover, strategic networkers don't just influence their relational environment; they shape it in their own image by moving and hiring subordinates, changing suppliers and sources of financing, lobbying to place allies in peer positions, and even restructuring their boards to create networks favorable to their business goals. Jody abjured such tactics, but her adversaries did not.

Strategic networking can be difficult for emerging leaders because it absorbs a significant amount of the time and energy that managers usually devote to meeting their many operational demands. This is one reason why many managers drop their strategic networking precisely when they need it most: when their units are in trouble and only outside support can rescue them. The trick is not to hide in the operational network but to develop it into a more strategic one.

One manager we studied, for example, used lateral and functional contacts throughout his firm to resolve tensions with his boss that resulted from substantial differences in style and strategic approaches between the two. Tied down in operational chores at a distant location, the manager had lost contact with headquarters. He resolved the situation by simultaneously obliging his direct reports to take on more of the local management effort and sending messages through his network that would help bring him back into the loop with the boss.

Operational, personal, and strategic networks are not mutually exclusive. One manager we studied used his personal passion, hunting, to meet people from professions as diverse as stonemasonry and household moving. Almost none of these hunting friends had anything to do with his work in the consumer electronics industry, yet they all had to deal with one of his own daily concerns: customer relations. Hearing about their problems and techniques allowed him to view his own from a different perspective and helped him define principles that he could test in his work. Ultimately, what began as a personal network of hunting partners became operationally and strategically valuable to this manager. The key was his ability to build inside-outside links for maximum leverage. But we've seen others who avoided networking, or failed at it, because they let interpersonal chemistry, not strategic needs, determine which relationships they cultivated.

Just Do It

The word "work" is part of networking, and it is not easy work, because it involves reaching outside the borders of a manager's comfort zone. How, then, can managers lessen the pain and increase the gain? The trick is to leverage the elements from each domain of networking into the others—to seek out personal contacts who can be objective, strategic counselors, for example, or to transform colleagues in adjacent functions into a constituency. Above all, many managers will need to change their attitudes about the legitimacy and necessity of networking.

Mind your mind-set

In our ongoing discussions with managers learning to improve their networking skills, we often hear, "That's all well and good, but I already have a day job." Others, like Jody, consider working through networks a way to rely on "whom you know" rather than "what you know"—a hypocritical, even unethical way to get things done. Whatever the reason, when aspiring leaders do not believe that networking is one of the most important requirements of their new jobs, they will not allocate enough time and effort to see it pay off.

The best solution we've seen to this trap is a good role model. Many times, what appears to be unpalatable or unproductive behavior takes on a new light when a person you respect does it well and ethically. For example, Gabriel Chenard, general manager for Europe of a group of consumer product brands, learned from the previous general manager how to take advantage of branch visits to solidify his relationships with employees and customers. Every flight and car trip became a venue for catching up and building relationships with the people who were accompanying him. Watching how much his boss got done on what would otherwise be downtime, Gabriel adopted the practice as a crucial part of his own management style. Networking effectively and ethically, like any other tacit skill, is a matter of judgment and intuition. We learn by observing and getting feedback from those for whom it's second nature.

Work from the outside in

One of the most daunting aspects of strategic networking is that there often seems to be no natural "excuse" for making contact with a more senior person outside one's function or business unit. It's difficult to build a relationship with anyone, let alone a senior executive, without a reason for interacting, like a common task or a shared purpose.

Some successful managers find common ground from the outside in—by, for instance, transposing a personal interest into the strategic domain. Linda Henderson is a good example. An investment banker responsible for a group of media industry clients, she always wondered how to connect to some of her senior colleagues who served other industries. She resolved to make time for an extracurricular passion—the theater—in a way that would enhance her business development activities. Four times a year, her secretary booked a buffet dinner at a downtown hotel and reserved a block of theater tickets. Key clients were invited. Through these events, Linda not only developed her own business but also learned about her clients' companies in a way that generated ideas for other parts of her firm, thus enabling her to engage with colleagues.

Other managers build outside-inside connections by using their functional interests or expertise. For example, communities of practice exist (or can easily be created on the Internet) in almost every area of business from brand management to Six Sigma to global strategy. Savvy managers reach out to kindred spirits outside their organizations to contribute and multiply their knowledge; the information they glean, in more cases than not, becomes the "hook" for making internal connections.

Re-allocate your time

If an aspiring leader has not yet mastered the art of delegation, he or she will find many reasons not to spend time networking. Participating in formal and informal meetings with people in other units takes time away from functional responsibilities and internal team affairs. Between the obvious payoff of a task accomplished and the ambiguous, often delayed rewards of networking, naive managers repeatedly choose the former. The less they practice networking, the less efficient at it they become, and the vicious cycle continues.

Henrik, the production manager and board member we described earlier, for example, did what he needed to do in order to prepare for board meetings but did not associate with fellow board members outside those formal events. As a result, he was frequently surprised when other board members raised issues at the heart of his role. In contrast, effective business leaders spend a lot of time every day gathering the information they need to meet their goals, relying on informal discussions with a lot of people who are not necessarily in charge of an issue or task. They network in order to obtain information continually, not just at formal meetings.

Ask and you shall receive

Many managers equate having a good network with having a large database of contacts, or attending high-profile professional conferences and events. In fact, we've seen people kick off a networking initiative by improving their record keeping or adopting a network management tool. But they falter at the next step—picking up the phone. Instead, they wait until they need something *badly*. The best networkers do exactly the opposite: They take every opportunity to give to, and receive from, the network, whether they need help or not.

A network lives and thrives only when it is used. A good way to begin is to make a simple request or take the initiative to connect two people who would benefit from meeting each other. Doing something—anything—gets the ball rolling and builds confidence that one does, in fact, have something to contribute.

Stick to it

It takes a while to reap the benefits of networking. We have seen many managers resolve to put networking at the top of their agendas, only to be derailed by the first crisis that comes along. One example is Harris Roberts, a regulatory affairs expert who realized he needed a broader network to achieve his goal of becoming a business unit manager. To force himself into what felt like an "unnatural act," Harris volunteered to be the liaison for his business school cohort's alumni network. But six months later, when a major new-drug approval process overwhelmed his calendar, Harris dropped all outside activities. Two years later, he found himself out of touch and still a functional manager. He failed to recognize that by not taking the time to attend industry conferences or compare notes with his peers, he was missing out on the strategic perspective and information that would make him a more attractive candidate for promotion.

Building a leadership network is less a matter of skill than of will. When first efforts do not bring quick rewards, some may simply conclude that networking isn't among their talents. But networking is not a talent; nor does it require a gregarious, extroverted personality. It is a skill, one that takes practice. We have seen over and over again that people who work at networking can learn not only how to do it well but also how to enjoy it. And they tend to be more successful in their careers than those who fail to leverage external ties or insist on defining their jobs narrowly.

Making a successful leadership transition requires a shift from the confines of a clearly defined operational network. Aspiring leaders must learn to build and use strategic networks that cross organizational and functional boundaries, and then link them up in novel and innovative ways. It is a challenge to make the leap from a lifetime of functional contributions and hands-on control to the ambiguous process of building and working through networks. Leaders must find new ways of defining themselves and develop new relationships to anchor and feed their emerging personas. They must also accept that networking is one of the most important requirements of their new leadership roles and continue to allocate enough time and effort to see it pay off.

Originally published in January 2007. Reprint R0701C

How to Bounce Back from Adversity

by Joshua D. Margolis and Paul G. Stoltz

THINGS ARE HUMMING ALONG, and then: A top client calls and says, "We're switching suppliers, starting next month. I'm afraid your company no longer figures into our plans." Or three colleagues, all of whom joined the organization around the same time you did, are up for promotion—but you aren't. Or your team loses another good person in a third round of layoffs; weak markets or no, you still need to make your numbers, but now you'll have to rely heavily on two of the most uncooperative members of the group.

So how do you react? Are you angry and disappointed, ranting and raving to anyone who will listen? Do you feel dejected and victimized, resigned to the situation even as you deny the cold reality of it? Or do you experience a rush of excitement—perhaps tinged with fear—because you sense an opportunity to develop your skills and talents in ways you'd never imagined? The truth is, you've probably reacted in all those ways when confronted with a challenge—maybe even cycling through multiple emotional states in the course of dealing with one really big mess.

Whatever your initial reaction, however, the challenge is to turn a negative experience into a productive one—that is, to counter adversity with resilience. Psychological resilience is the capacity to respond quickly and constructively to crises. It's a central dynamic in most survival stories, such as those of the shell-shocked individuals and organizations that rallied in the wake of 9/11 and Hurricane Katrina. But resilience can be hard to muster for many reasons: Fear, anger, and confusion can paralyze us after a severe setback. Assigning blame rather than generating solutions is an all-too-human tendency. Worse yet, those to whom we turn for counsel may offer us exactly the wrong kind of advice.

Decades of research in psychology, on topics including hardiness, learned helplessness, coping, and the correlation between cognitive style and health, confirms that each of us has a distinct, consistent pattern of thinking about life's twists and turns—a pattern of which most of us are largely unaware. It may be an unconscious reflex to look backward from traumatic incidents to explain what just happened. Such analysis can be useful, certainly—but only up to the point where strong negative emotions start to prevent our moving on.

We believe that managers can build high levels of resilience in themselves and their teams by taking charge of how they think about adversity. Resilient managers move quickly from analysis to a plan of action (and reaction). After the onset of adversity, they shift from cause-oriented thinking to response-oriented thinking, and their focus is strictly forward. In our work with leaders in a variety of companies and industries, we've identified four lenses through which managers can view adverse events to make this shift effectively.

- **Control.** When a crisis hits, do you look for what you can improve now rather than trying to identify all the factors—even those beyond your control—that caused it in the first place?

- **Impact.** Can you sidestep the temptation to find the origins of the problem in yourself or others and focus instead on identifying what positive effects your personal actions might have?

- **Breadth.** Do you assume that the underlying cause of the crisis is specific and can be contained, or do you worry that it might cast a long shadow over all aspects of your life?

- **Duration.** How long do you believe that the crisis and its repercussions will last?

Idea in Brief

Psychological resilience—the capacity to respond quickly and constructively in a crisis—can be hard to muster when a manager is paralyzed by fear, anger, confusion, or a tendency to assign blame.

Resilient managers shift quickly from endlessly dissecting traumatic events to looking forward, determining the best course of action given new realities. They understand the size and scope of the crisis and the levels of control and impact they may have in a bad situation.

The authors describe a **resilience regimen**—a series of pointed questions designed to help managers replace negative responses with creative, resourceful ones and to move forward despite real or perceived obstacles.

The first two lenses characterize an individual's personal reaction to adversity, and the second two capture his or her impressions of the adversity's magnitude. Managers should consider all four to fully understand their instinctive responses to personal and professional challenges, setbacks, or failures.

In the following pages we'll describe a deliberative rather than reflexive approach to dealing with hardship—what we call a *resilience regimen*. By asking a series of pointed questions, managers can grasp their own and their direct reports' habits of thought and help reframe negative events in productive ways. With the four lenses as a guide, they can learn to stop feeling paralyzed by crisis, respond with strength and creativity, and help their direct reports do the same.

When Adversity Strikes

Most of us go with our gut when something bad happens. Deeply ingrained habits and beliefs sap our energy and keep us from acting constructively. People commonly fall into one of two emotional traps. One is *deflation*. Someone who has marched steadily through a string of successes can easily come to feel like a hero, able to fix any problem single-handedly. A traumatic event can snap that person back to reality. Even for the less heroic among us, adversity can touch off intense bursts of negative emotion—as if a dark cloud had settled behind our eyes, as one manager described it. We may feel disappointed in ourselves or others, mistreated and dispirited, even besieged.

That was the case with an executive we'll call Andrea, who headed up a major subsidiary of a U.S. automotive parts supplier. She had put up with years of internal bickering and the company's calcified cost structure. But over time she managed to bring the warring factions—unions, management, engineers, and marketers—together, and she gained widespread approval for a plan that would phase out old facilities and reduce crippling costs: Rather than try to supply every make and manufacturer, the company would focus on the truck market. Even more important, Andrea rallied everyone around a new line of products and a clear value proposition for customers that would rejuvenate the company's brand. The future looked bright.

Then fuel prices skyrocketed, the economy seized up, and demand from all segments of the truck market evaporated almost overnight. The recession had brought unfathomable challenges to the organization, and their suddenness left Andrea feeling as if she'd been socked in the stomach. After all her hard work, difficult conversations, and strategizing to fix the previous problems, she felt overmatched—for the first time in her career. Andrea lacked resilience precisely because she had a long history of wins.

The other emotional trap is *victimization*. Many of us assume the role of helpless bystander in the face of an adverse event. "Those people" have put us in an unfortunate position, we tell ourselves (and others) again and again. We dismiss both criticism and helpful suggestions from others, and go out of our way to affirm that we're right, everyone else is wrong, and no one understands us. Meanwhile, self-doubt may creep in, making us feel hopelessly constrained by circumstances.

Greg, a senior business development manager at an electronic accessories company, felt just this way. He had sailed through his first three years at the company with several promotions, taking on increasing responsibility—first for building brand awareness among younger consumers, and then for building new relationships (and gaining more shelf space) with large retailers throughout the United States and Canada. But as global competition heated up, Greg's peers and superiors asked him to rethink his approach and questioned whether retail outlets were still a viable distribution channel. Big-box stores were squeezing the company's margins, and physically servicing all the company's accounts seemed unnecessarily expensive compared with online options. Greg reacted to his colleagues' requests by becoming more and more defensive and extremely angry.

These stories illustrate the two-headed hydra of contemporary adversity. First, highly accomplished managers are confronting, in rapid succession, challenges the likes of which they've never seen before—a worldwide economic crisis, the globalization of business, the rise of new technologies, deep demographic shifts. Feeling discouraged and helpless, they turn away from the problem and, unfortunately, from people who might be able to help. Second, even if these managers went to their bosses for guidance, they'd most likely receive inadequate coaching. That's because most supervisors, riding their own long wave of hard-won successes, lack the empathy to intervene effectively. They may not know how to counsel direct reports they feel aren't quite as talented as they were at escaping the shadow of defeat. They may be so well accustomed to handling adversity in ways that minimize their psychological stress that they don't recognize their own bad habits. (See the sidebar "Coaching Resilience.")

The Capacity for Resilience

Independent studies in psychology and our own observations suggest that the ability to bounce back from adversity hinges on uncovering and untangling one's implicit beliefs about it—and shifting how one responds.

Most of us, when we experience a difficult episode, make quick assumptions about its causes, magnitude, consequences, and duration. We instantly decide, for example, whether it was inevitable, a function of forces beyond our control, or whether we could somehow have prevented it. Managers need to shift from this kind of reflexive thinking to "active" thinking about how best to respond,

Coaching Resilience

OFTEN EVEN THE MOST RESILIENT MANAGERS run into trouble trying to coach direct reports in crisis. They react with either a how-to pep talk delivered utterly without empathy or understanding, or a sympathetic ear and reassurance that things will turn out OK. Neither response will equip your team members to handle the next unforeseen twist or turn. Instead, you should adopt a collaborative, inquisitive approach that can help your direct reports generate their own options and possibilities.

Suppose a defensive employee were self-aware enough to ask you, his mentor, for help dealing with a professional setback—say, being passed over for promotion. You could just acknowledge his feelings and basically manage his response for him—outlining who he needs to talk to and in what order, and what to do if he doesn't get the answers he wants. But if you ask specifying, visualizing, and collaborating questions—such as "How can you step up to make the most immediate, positive impact on this situation?" and "How do you think your efforts in that direction would affect your team and your peers?"—you put the ball back in your employee's court. You're not endorsing any particular perspective, you're not providing absolute answers—you're helping to build resilience in a team member.

---

asking themselves what aspects they can control, what impact they can have, and how the breadth and duration of the crisis might be contained. Three types of questions can help them make this shift.

Specifying questions help managers identify ways to intervene; the more specific the answers, the better. *Visualizing questions* help shift their attention away from the adverse event and toward a more positive outcome. *Collaborating questions* push them to reach out to others—not for affirmation or commiseration but for joint problem solving. Each type of question can clarify each of the four lenses of resilient thinking.

Taken together, the four sets make up the resilience regimen. Let's take a closer look at each set in turn.

Control

According to multiple studies—including those by Bernard Weiner, of UCLA, and James Amirkhan, of Cal State Long Beach, and the classic University of Chicago study of executives by Suzanne Ouellette and Salvatore Maddi—our reactions to stressful situations depend on the degree of control we believe we can exercise. Andrea struggled with whether she could still contribute meaningfully to her company or whether the sudden shifts in the economy had moved the situation beyond her control. If Greg continued to attribute criticism of his retail strategy to "scheming peers," he might fail to see what he personally could do to influence the company's long-term strategy or his own destiny. The following questions can help managers identify ways to exercise control over what happens next:

Specifying: What aspects of the situation can I directly influence to change the course of this adverse event?

Visualizing: What would the manager I most admire do in this situation?

Collaborating: Who on my team can help me, and what's the best way to engage that person or those people?

The goal in asking these questions is not to come up with a final plan of action or an immediate understanding of how the team should react. Rather, it is to generate possibilities—to develop, in a disciplined and concrete way, an inventory of what *might* be done. (The next set of questions can help managers outline what *will* be done.) Had Andrea asked herself these three questions, she might have identified an opportunity to, say, rally the company around emerging safety and fuel-efficiency devices in the industry, or to use the slowdown to perfect the company's newer, still-promising products by working more closely with major customers. Similarly, if Greg had undertaken the exercise, he might have been able to channel something his mentor once told him: "It's not about whether I'm right or wrong. It's about what's best for the company." With that in mind, Greg might have clearly seen the benefits of reaching out to his peers and team members to assess alternative go-to-market approaches. The ingenuity and work ethic he had applied to building the retail business could have been turned to devising the next great strategy.

Impact

Related to our beliefs about whether we can turn things around are our assumptions about what caused a negative event: Did the problem originate with us personally, or somewhere else? Greg attributed the criticism of his retail distribution strategy to his "competitive, power-hungry" colleagues rather than to the possible shortcomings of his approach. He was too deeply mired in defensiveness to get out of his own way. Andrea felt powerless in the face of challenges she'd never before had to meet and forces that eclipsed her individual initiative and effort. Instead of giving in to deflation and victimization, managers can focus intently on how they might affect the event's outcome.

Specifying: How can I step up to make the most immediate, positive impact on this situation?

Visualizing: What positive effect might my efforts have on those around me?

Collaborating: How can I mobilize the efforts of those who are hanging back?

If he had focused on these questions, Greg might have seen that he was not simply being asked to discard his accounts and acknowledge that his strategy was misguided; rather, he was being cast as a potential player in the organization's change efforts. He might have appreciated that openly and rigorously assessing his business-development strategy could influence others—whether his assessment validated the status quo or led to a solution no one had thought of yet. And he might have reignited the entrepreneurial culture he so valued when he joined the company by soliciting others' input on the marketing strategy. For her part, Andrea knew all too well that her company's fortunes depended on economic conditions—but she couldn't see how her response to the market failures might energize the organization. These questions might have helped her.

Breadth

When we encounter a setback, we tend to assume that its causes are either specific to the situation or more broadly applicable, like poison that will taint everything we touch. To build up resilience, managers need to stop worrying about the reach of the causes and focus instead on how to limit the damage. These questions may even highlight opportunities in the midst of chaos.

A Change in Mind-Set

TO STRENGTHEN THEIR RESILIENCE, managers need to shift from reflexive, cause-oriented thinking to active, response-oriented thinking.

Cause-oriented thinking	Response-oriented thinking
CONTROL	
Was this adverse event inevitable, or could I have prevented it?	What features of the situation can I (even potentially) improve?
IMPACT	
Did I cause the adverse event, or did it result from external sources?	What sort of positive impact can I personally have on what happens next?
BREADTH	
Is the underlying cause of this event specific to it or more widespread?	How can I contain the negatives of the situation and generate currently unseen positives?
DURATION	
Is the underlying cause of this event enduring or temporary?	What can I do to begin addressing the problem now?

Specifying: What can I do to reduce the potential downside of this adverse event—by even 10%? What can I do to maximize the potential upside—by even 10%?

Visualizing: What strengths and resources will my team and I develop by addressing this event?

Collaborating: What can each of us do on our own, and what can we do collectively, to contain the damage and transform the situation into an opportunity?

These questions might have helped Andrea achieve two core objectives. Instead of endlessly revisiting the repercussions of plummeting truck sales, she might have identified large and small ways in which she and her team could use the economic crisis to reconfigure the company's manufacturing processes. And rather than fixating on how awful and extensive the damage to the organization was, she could have imagined a new postrecession norm—thriving in the face of tighter resources, more selective customers, and more exacting government scrutiny. Greg might have seen that he had a rare opportunity to gain valuable leadership skills and relevant insights about competitors' marketing strategies by engaging peers and team members in reassessing the retail strategy.

Duration

Some hardships in the workplace seem to have no end in sight—underperformance quarter after quarter, recurring clashes between people at different levels and in different parts of the company, a stalled economy. But questions about duration can put the brakes on such runaway nightmares. Here, though, it's important to begin by imagining the desired outcome.

Visualizing: What do I want life to look like on the other side of this adversity?

Specifying: What can I do in the next few minutes, or hours, to move in that direction?

Collaborating: What sequence of steps can we put together as a team, and what processes can we develop and adopt, to see us through to the other side of this hardship?

Greg was sure that criticism of his business-development approach signaled the end: no more promotions, no more recognition from higher-ups of his hard work and tangible results, nothing to look forward to but doing others' bidding in a company that was sowing the seeds of decline. These three questions might have broadened his outlook. That is, he might have seen the benefits of quickly arranging meetings with his mentor (for personal counsel) and with his team (for professional input on strategy). The questions could have been a catalyst for listing the data required to make a case for or against change, the analyses the team would need to run, and the questions about various sales channels and approaches that needed to be answered. This exercise might have helped Greg see a workable path through the challenge he was experiencing. The result would have been renewed confidence that he and his team could keep their company at the forefront of customer service.

The Research Behind the
Resilience Regimen

TWO CONVERGING STREAMS OF RESEARCH informed our work. The first examines how patterns of understanding the world shape people's responses to stressful situations. Albert Ellis and Aaron Beck pioneered this research, followed by, among others, Martin Seligman and Christopher Peterson on learned helplessness; Richard Lazarus and Susan Folkman on coping; and Lyn Abramson, David Burns, and James Amirkhan on how "attributional styles" affect health. More recently, Karen Reivich and Andrew Shatté identified how people can strengthen their resilience.

The second stream, pioneered by Suzanne Ouellette and Salvatore Maddi in their studies of hardiness and extended most recently by Deborah Khoshaba and Aaron Antonovsky, explored what differentiated two groups of people who encountered intense stress. One group flourished while the other sank.

A common finding emerges from these two streams of inquiry: How people approach trying circumstances influences both their ability to deal with them and, ultimately, their own success and well-being.

Answering the Questions

Although the question sets offer a useful framework for retraining managers' responses, simply knowing what to ask isn't enough. You won't become more resilient simply because you've read this far and have made a mental note to pull out these questions the next time a destabilizing difficulty strikes. To strengthen your capacity for resilience, you need to internalize the questions by following two simple precepts:

Write down the answers
Various studies on stress and coping with trauma demonstrate that the act of writing about difficult episodes can enhance an individual's emotional and physical well-being. Indeed, writing offers people command over an adverse situation in a way that merely thinking about it does not. It's best to treat the resilience regimen as a timed exercise: Give yourself at least 15 minutes, uninterrupted, to write

down your responses to the 12 questions. That may seem both too long and too short—too long because managers rarely have that much time for any activity, let alone one involving personal reflection. But you'll actually end up saving time. Instead of ruminating about events, letting them interrupt your work, you'll have solutions in the making. As you come to appreciate and rely on this exercise, 15 minutes may feel too short.

Do it every day

When you're learning any new skill, repetition is critical. The resilience regimen is a long-term fitness plan, not a crash diet. You must ask and answer these questions daily if they are to become second nature. But that can't happen if bad habits crowd out the questions. You don't need to experience a major trauma to practice; you can ask yourself the questions in response to daily annoyances that sap your energy—a delayed flight, a slow computer, an unresponsive colleague. You can use the four lenses in virtually any order, but it's important to start with your weakest dimension. If you tend to blame others and overlook your own potential to contribute, start with the impact questions. If you tend to worry that the adverse event will ruin everything, start with the breadth questions.

Under ongoing duress, executives' capacity for resilience is critical to maintaining their mental and physical health. Paradoxically, however, building resilience is best done precisely when times are most difficult—when we face the most upending challenges, when we are at the greatest risk of misfiring with our reactions, when we are blindest to the opportunities presented. All the more reason, then, to use the resilience regimen to tamp down unproductive responses to adversity, replace negativity with creativity and resourcefulness, and get things done despite real or perceived obstacles.

Originally published in January–February 2010. Reprint R1001E

Rebounding from Career Setbacks

by Mitchell Lee Marks, Philip Mirvis, and Ron Ashkenas

BRIAN WAS A RISING STAR at his company. He advanced through several senior management roles and was soon tapped to head a business unit, reporting directly to the CEO. But after about two years in the job, despite his stellar financial results, his boss suddenly dismissed him. Brian was told that the company was trying to be a more open, engaged, global enterprise and that his aggressive leadership style didn't reflect those values.

Like most ambitious managers who suffer career setbacks, Brian went through a period of shock, denial, and self-doubt. After all, he'd never previously failed in a position. He had trouble accepting the reality that he wasn't as good as he'd thought he was. He also felt upset and angry that his boss hadn't given him a chance to prove himself. Eventually, however, he recognized that he couldn't reverse the decision and chose to focus on moving forward. None of the people working for him had objected to his dismissal, so he was particularly keen to figure out how to foster loyalty in future employees.

Within a few months, a large industrial parts company impressed with Brian's undisputed ability to meet financial targets recruited him to lead a division. The job was a step down from his previous role, but he decided to take it so that he could experiment with different ways of working and leading, learning to better control his emotions and rally his team around him. It paid off: Less than three years later, yet another company—this time, a *Fortune* 500 manufacturer—hired him to be its CEO. During his seven-year tenure in that job, he doubled the firm's revenue and created a culture that balanced innovation with a disciplined focus on productivity and performance.

Of course, not everyone can go from being out of a job to running a large company. But in more than 30 years of research and consulting work with executive clients, we've found that one lesson from Brian's story applies pretty universally: Even a dramatic career failure can become a springboard to success if you respond in the right way. To execute a turnaround like Brian's, you focus on a few key tasks: Determine why you lost, identify new paths, and seize the right opportunity when it's within your reach.

Figure Out Why You Lost

We've interviewed hundreds of executives who have been fired, laid off, or passed over for promotion (as a result of mergers, restructurings, competition for top jobs, or personal failings). Often, we find them working through the classic stages of loss defined by psychiatrist Elisabeth Kübler-Ross: They start with shock and denial about the events and move on to anger at the company or the boss, bargaining over their fate, and then a protracted period of licking their wounds and asking themselves whether they can ever regain the respect of their peers and team. Many of them never make it to the "acceptance" stage.

That's partly because, as social psychologists have found in decades' worth of studies, high achievers usually take too much credit for their successes and assign too much external blame for their failures. It's a type of attribution bias that protects self-esteem but also prevents learning and growth. People focus on situational factors or company politics instead of examining their own role in the problem.

Some ask others for candid feedback, but most turn to sympathetic friends, family members, and colleagues who reinforce their self-image ("You deserved that job") and feed their sense of injustice

("You have every right to be angry"). This prevents them from considering their own culpability and breaking free of the destructive behavior that derailed them in the first place. It may also lead them to ratchet back their current efforts and future expectations in the workplace.

Those who rebound from career losses take a decidedly different approach. Instead of getting stuck in grief or blame, they actively explore how they contributed to what went wrong, evaluate whether they sized up the situation correctly and reacted appropriately, and consider what they would do differently if given the chance. They also gather feedback from a wide variety of people (including superiors, peers, and subordinates), making it clear that they want honest feedback, not consolation.

Brian, for example, had to engage in frank, somewhat painful conversations with his boss, several direct reports, and a few trusted colleagues to discover that he had developed a career-limiting reputation for being difficult and not always in control of his emotions.

Also consider Stan, a senior partner at a boutique professional services firm considering global expansion. A vocal proponent of the growth plan, he had hoped to lead the company's new London office. When another partner was selected instead, Stan was outraged. He stewed for a few weeks but then resolved to take a more productive tack. He set up one-on-one meetings with members of the firm's executive committee. At the start of each session, he explained that he wasn't trying to reverse the decision; he just wanted to understand why it had been made. He took care not to sound bitter or to bad-mouth the process or the people involved. He maintained a positive, confident tone, and he expressed a willingness to learn from his missteps.

As a result, the executive committee members gave him consistent, useful comments: They regarded his aggressiveness as an asset in the United States but worried that it would get in the way of securing new clients and running an office in the UK. His initial reaction was defensive. ("No one minded my aggressiveness when it landed key contracts," he thought.) But he kept those feelings in check—and quickly came around to appreciating the candor. "It wasn't that they were asking me to change," Stan reflected, "but they made clear to me that my style got in the way of this opportunity."

Identify New Paths

The next step is to objectively weight the potential for turning your loss into a win, whether that's a different role in your organization, a move to a new company, or a shift to a different industry or career.

Reframing losses as opportunities involves hard thinking about who you are and what you want. Research shows that escapism is a common reaction to career derailment—people may take trips to get away from their troubles, immerse themselves in busywork, drink or eat excessively, or avoid discussing their thoughts and plans with family and friends. While these behaviors can give you mental space to sort things out, they rarely lead to a productive transition. It's more effective to engage in a focused exploration of all the options available.

New opportunities don't usually present themselves right away, of course, and it can be hard to spot them through the fog of anger and disappointment in the early days after a setback. Studies by change management expert William Bridges highlight the tension people feel when they're torn between hanging onto their current identities and expectations and letting go. Leaders we've counseled describe entering a "twilight zone": The status quo has been fatally disrupted, but it's not clear yet what success will look like in the future.

That's why it's useful to take time to test out some ideas for what to do next. One option is to speak with a career counselor or engage in therapy, both to clarify goals and to work on personal development. Another is to take a temporary leave from your job to go back to school or test-drive a career interest at a start-up or a nonprofit. Pausing a bit can allow you to find new meaning in your setback.

Recall how Brian reacted when he was fired from his unit-head job: He began to consider lower-level positions that would give him room to tinker with his leadership style. Or look at Paula, whom we met while studying the resiliency of online advertising executives involved in restructurings. When her high-tech company's new CEO launched a corporate makeover, Paula felt relatively safe because the European business unit she led had met or exceeded its targets for 11 straight quarters, and she had been promoted three times in five years. But then she discovered that her position would be eliminated.

At first Paula blamed everything from company politics to her boss's failure to protect her and her team. Then, three months after the announcement, her last day arrived. She had no plans and didn't want to make any right away. Instead she spent time examining her life and her career. She reached out to friends and business associates—"not to network" (her words) but to gain perspective and advice in thinking through her goals. She reflected on each conversation, made notes, and eventually developed what she dubbed "four themes for my next job": She wanted to bring new products to market (rather than relaunching U.S. offerings in other regions), to interact more directly with clients, to work for a company with a unique value proposition, and to have colleagues she liked and trusted. Paula then tailored her job search to achieve those goals.

Seize the Right Opportunity

After you identify possible next steps, it's time to pick one. Admittedly, this can be a little frightening, especially if you're venturing into unknown career territory. Reimagining your professional identity is one thing; bringing it to life is another. Remember, though, that you haven't left your skills and experience behind with your last job, and you'll also bring with you the lessons learned from the setback. You may also have productively revised your definition of success.

Research we've conducted, along with career specialist Douglas (Tim) Hall, shows that needs and priorities can change dramatically over time—as children are born or grow up and move out, after a divorce or a parent's death, when early dreams fade in midlife and new ones emerge, and when perspectives and skills become outdated and new growth challenges beckon. So choosing the right opportunity has a lot to do with the moment when you happen to be looking.

Paula's story is a case in point. Her list of "must haves" led her to interview for and accept a more senior position, as VP of international sales, at a smaller firm in the same industry. The job was located in the European city where she already lived and wanted to stay.

Brian, by contrast, took a significant step down, but he took advantage of the opportunity to learn to become a better manager. He developed an understanding of the triggers that had caused him to behave unproductively in the past and devised coping strategies. For example, instead of immediately pouncing on subordinates for performance "misses," he learned to have off-line discussions with the relevant managers. After some practice, the measured approach began to feel more natural to him.

Bruce, a senior IT manager at a New York bank that went through a merger, is another example. He kept his job in the deal's aftermath but was devastated to lose out in his bid to become the chief technology officer of the merged company. He stayed on through the integration, but after a year of rethinking his personal and career goals—and considering a variety of jobs—he moved with his family to Austin, Texas, and joined a small technology firm that became wildly successful. Just as important, he also found time to coach his two children's soccer teams and pursue his passion for music as a guitarist for a local band.

Like Paula and Brian, Bruce did serious discovery work after his setback—and then acted with conviction. He moved to a new city, industry, and job that would allow him to recover and thrive.

For executives who decide to stay with their employers, the biggest change may be in mind-set or psychological commitment. That's what happened with Stan at the professional services firm: Having gained a clearer sense of how his colleagues viewed him, he embraced his role as rainmaker, better appreciating the income, status, and perks that came with it. He also found a new source of satisfaction and accomplishment: mentoring the next generation of talent on how to win new business.

Shifting perspective like this takes just as much energy as switching companies or jobs. If you're not able to dig into your current work with renewed gusto, as Stan did, you might decide to put more discretionary effort into family life, volunteering, or hobbies, recognizing that having a rich personal life can compensate for not being number one on your team or in your organization.

———————

We all know the importance of resilience and adaptability when it comes to career success. But these qualities don't come easily or naturally to everyone, which is why it's so useful to have clear steps to follow after a setback. The approach laid out here can help transform the anger and self-doubt associated with failure into excitement about new possibilities.

Originally published in October 2014. Reprint R1410J

Reawakening Your Passion for Work

by Richard Boyatzis, Annie McKee, and Daniel Goleman

LAST SEPTEMBER, as millions of people around the globe stared in disbelief at television screens, watching the World Trade Center towers crumble to the ground, many of us realized that accompanying the shock and sorrow was another sensation—the impulse to take stock. The fragile nature of human life, exposed with such unbearable clarity, compelled people to ask a haunting question: "Am I really living the way I want to live?"

We all struggle with the question of personal meaning throughout our lives. September 11, 2001, brought the issue into focus for many people all at once, but the impulse to take stock comes up periodically for most of us in far less dramatic circumstances. The senior executives who read this magazine, for instance, seem to struggle with this question at the high point of their careers. Why? Many executives hit their professional stride in their forties and fifties, just as their parents are reaching the end of their lives—a reminder that all of us are mortal. What's more, many of the personality traits associated with career success, such as a knack for problem solving and sheer tenacity, lead people to stick with a difficult situation in the hope of making it better. Then one day, a creeping sensation sets in: Something is wrong. That realization launches a process we have witnessed—literally thousands of times—in our work coaching managers and executives over the past 14 years.

The process is rarely easy, but we've found this type of awakening to be healthy and necessary; leaders need to go through it every few years to replenish their energy, creativity, and commitment—and to rediscover their passion for work and life. Indeed, leaders cannot keep achieving new goals and inspiring the people around them without understanding their own dreams. In this article, we'll look at the different signals that it's time to take stock—whether you have a nagging sense of doubt that builds over time until it's impossible to ignore or you experience a life-changing event that irrevocably alters your perspective. Then we'll describe some strategies for listening to those signals and taking restorative action. Such action can range from a relatively minor adjustment in outlook, to a larger refocusing on what really matters, to practical life changes that take you in an entirely new direction.

When to Say When

When asked, most businesspeople say that passion—to lead, to serve the customer, to support a cause or a product—is what drives them. When that passion fades, they begin to question the meaning of their work. How can you reawaken the passion and reconnect with what's meaningful for you? The first step is acknowledging the signal that it's time to take stock. Let's look at the various feelings that let you know the time has come.

"I feel trapped"

Sometimes, a job that was fulfilling gradually becomes less meaningful, slowly eroding your enthusiasm and spirit until you no longer find much purpose in your work. People often describe this state as feeling trapped. They're restless, yet they can't seem to change—or even articulate what's wrong.

Take the case of Bob McDowell, the corporate director of human resources at a large professional-services firm. After pouring his heart and soul into his work for 25 years, Bob had become terribly demoralized because his innovative programs were cut time and again. As a result, his efforts could do little to improve the workplace over the long

Idea in Brief

All of us struggle from time to time with the question of personal meaning: "Am I living the way I want to live?" This type of questioning is healthy; business leaders need to go through it every few years to replenish their energy, creativity, and commitment—and their passion for work. In this article, the authors describe the signals that it's time to reevaluate your choices and illuminate strategies for responding to those signals. Such wake-up calls come in various forms. Some people feel trapped or bored and may realize that they have adjusted to the frustrations of their work to such an extent that they barely recognize themselves. For others, the signal comes when they are faced with an ethical challenge or suddenly discover their true calling. Once you have realized that it's time to take stock of your life, there are strategies to help you consider where you are, where you're headed, and where you want to be. Many people find that calling a time-out—either in the form of an intense, soul-searching exercise or a break from corporate life—is the best way to reconnect with their dreams. People no longer expect their leaders to have all the answers, but they do expect them to try to keep their own passion alive and to support employees through that process.

term. For years he had quieted his nagging doubts, in part because an occasional success or a rare employee who flourished under his guidance provided deep, if temporary, satisfaction. Moreover, the job carried all the usual trappings of success—title, money, and perks. And, like most people in middle age, McDowell had financial responsibilities that made it risky to trade security for personal fulfillment. Factors such as these conspire to keep people trudging along, hoping things will get better. But clinging to security or trying to be a good corporate citizen can turn out to be a prison of your own making.

"I'm bored"

Many people confuse achieving day-to-day business goals with performing truly satisfying work, so they continue setting and achieving new goals—until it dawns on them that they are bored. People are often truly shaken by this revelation; they feel as if they have just emerged from a spiritual blackout. We saw this in Nick Mimken, the owner of a successful insurance agency, who increasingly felt that something was missing from his life. He joined a book group, hoping that intellectual stimulation would help him regain some enthusiasm, but it wasn't enough. The fact was, he had lost touch with his dreams and was going through the motions at work without experiencing any real satisfaction from the success of his business.

High achievers like Mimken may have trouble accepting that they're bored because it's often the generally positive traits of ambition and determination to succeed that obscure the need for fun. Some people may feel guilty about being restless when it looks like they have it all. Others may admit they aren't having fun but believe that's the price of success. As one manager said, "I work to live. I don't expect to find deep meaning at the office; I get that elsewhere." The problem? Like many, this man works more than 60 hours a week, leaving him little time to enjoy anything else.

"I'm not the person I want to be"

Some people gradually adjust to the letdowns, frustrations, and even boredom of their work until they surrender to a routine that's incompatible with who they are and what they truly want. Consider, for instance, John Lauer, an inspirational leader who took over as president of BFGoodrich and quickly captured the support of top executives with his insight into the company's challenges and opportunities, and his contagious passion for the business.

But after he'd been with the company about six years, we watched Lauer give a speech to a class of executive MBA students and saw that he had lost his spark. Over time, Lauer had fallen in step with a corporate culture that was focused on shareholder value in a way that was inconsistent with what he cared about. Not surprisingly, he left the company six months later, breaking from corporate life by joining his wife in her work with Hungarian relief organizations. He later admitted that he knew he wasn't himself by the end of his time at BFGoodrich, although he didn't quite know why.

How did Lauer stray from his core? First, the change was so gradual that he didn't notice that he was being absorbed into a culture that didn't fit him. Second, like many, he did what he felt he "should," going along with the bureaucracy and making minor concession after minor concession rather than following his heart. Finally, he exhibited a trait that is a hallmark of effective leaders: adaptability. At first, adapting to the corporate culture probably made Lauer feel more comfortable. But without strong self-awareness, people risk adapting to such an extent that they no longer recognize themselves.

"I won't compromise my ethics"

The signal to take stock may come to people in the form of a challenge to what they feel is right. Such was the case for Niall FitzGerald, now the cochairman of Unilever, when he was asked to take a leadership role in South Africa, which was still operating under apartheid. The offer was widely considered a feather in his cap and a positive sign about his future with Unilever. Until that time, FitzGerald had accepted nearly every assignment, but the South Africa opportunity stopped him in his tracks, posing a direct challenge to his principles. How could he, in good conscience, accept a job in a country whose political and practical environment he found reprehensible?

Or consider the case of a manager we'll call Rob. After working for several supportive and loyal bosses, he found himself reporting to an executive—we'll call him Martin—whose management style was in direct conflict with Rob's values. The man's abusive treatment of subordinates had derailed a number of promising careers, yet he was something of a legend in the company. To Rob's chagrin, the senior executive team admired Martin's performance and, frankly, felt that young managers benefited from a stint under his marine lieutenant-style leadership.

When you recognize that an experience is in conflict with your values, as FitzGerald and Rob did, you can at least make a conscious choice about how to respond. The problem is, people often miss this particular signal because they lose sight of their core values. Sometimes they separate their work from their personal lives to such an extent that they don't bring their values to the office. As a result, they may accept or even engage in behaviors they'd deem unacceptable at home. Other people find that their work *becomes* their life, and business goals take precedence over everything else. Many executives who genuinely value family above all still end up working

12-hour days, missing more and more family dinners as they pursue success at work. In these cases, people may not hear the wake-up call. Even if they do, they may sense that something isn't quite right but be unable to identify it—or do anything to change it.

"I can't ignore the call"

A wake-up call can come in the form of a mission: an irresistible force that compels people to step out, step up, and take on a challenge. It is as if they suddenly recognize what they are meant to do and cannot ignore it any longer.

Such a call is often spiritual, as in the case of the executive who, after examining his values and personal vision, decided to quit his job, become ordained, buy a building, and start a church—all at age 55. But a call can take other forms as well—to become a teacher, to work with disadvantaged children, or to make a difference to the people you encounter every day. Rebecca Yoon, who runs a dry-cleaning business, has come to consider it her mission to connect with her customers on a personal level. Her constant and sincere attention has created remarkable loyalty to her shop, even though the actual service she provides is identical to that delivered by hundreds of other dry cleaners in the city.

"Life is too short!"

Sometimes it takes a trauma, large or small, to jolt people into taking a hard look at their lives. Such an awakening may be the result of a heart attack, the loss of a loved one, or a world tragedy. It can also be the result of something less dramatic, like adjusting to an empty nest or celebrating a significant birthday. Priorities can become crystal clear at times like these, and things that seemed important weeks, days, or even minutes ago no longer matter.

For example, following a grueling and heroic escape from his office at One World Trade Center last September, John Paul DeVito of the May Davis Group stumbled into a church in tears, desperate to call his family. When a police officer tried to calm him down, DeVito responded, "I'm not in shock. I've never been more cognizant in my life." Even as he mourned the deaths of friends and colleagues, he continued to be ecstatic about life, and he's now reframing his priorities, amazed that before this horrific experience he put duty to his job above almost everything else.

DeVito is not alone. Anecdotal evidence suggests that many people felt the need to seek new meaning in their lives after the tragedies of last September, which highlighted the fact that life can be cut short at any time. An article in the December 26, 2001, *Wall Street Journal* described two women who made dramatic changes after the attacks. Following a visit to New York shortly after the towers were hit, engineer Betty Roberts quit her job at age 52 to enroll in divinity school. And Chicki Wentworth decided to give up the office and restaurant building she had owned and managed for nearly 30 years in order to work with troubled teens.

But as we've said, people also confront awakening events throughout their lives in much more mundane circumstances. Turning 40, getting married, sending a child to college, undergoing surgery, facing retirement—these are just a handful of the moments in life when we naturally pause, consider where our choices have taken us, and check our accomplishments against our dreams.

Interestingly, it's somehow more socially acceptable to respond to shocking or traumatic events than to any of the others. As a result, people who feel trapped and bored often stick with a job that's making them miserable for far too long, and thus they may be more susceptible to stress-related illnesses. What's more, the quieter signals—a sense of unease that builds over time, for example—can be easy to miss or dismiss because their day-to-day impact is incremental. But such signals are no less important as indicators of the need to reassess than the more visible events. How do you learn to listen to vital signals and respond before it's too late? It takes a conscious, disciplined effort at periodic self-examination.

Strategies for Renewal

There's no one-size-fits-all solution for restoring meaning and passion to your life. However, there are strategies for assessing your life and making corrections if you've gotten off course. Most people pursue not a single strategy but a combination, and some seek outside help while others prefer a more solitary journey. Regardless of which path you choose, you need time for reflection—a chance to consider where you are, where you're going, and where you really want to be. Let's look at five approaches.

Call a time-out

For some people, taking time off is the best way to figure out what they really want to do and to reconnect with their dreams. Academic institutions have long provided time for rejuvenation through sabbaticals—six to 12 months off, often with pay. Some businesses—to be clear, very few—offer sabbaticals as well, letting people take a paid leave to pursue their interests with the guarantee of a job when they return. More often, businesspeople who take time off do so on their own time—a risk, to be sure, but few who have stepped off the track regret the decision.

This is the path Bob McDowell took. McDowell, the HR director we described earlier who felt trapped in his job, stepped down from his position, did not look for another job, and spent about eight months taking stock of his life. He considered his successes and failures, and faced up to the sacrifices he had made by dedicating himself so completely to a job that was, in the end, less than fulfilling. Other executives take time off with far less ambitious goals—simply to get their heads out of their work for a while and focus on their personal lives. After a time, they may very happily go back to the work they'd been doing for years, eager to embrace the same challenges with renewed passion.

Still others might want to step off the fast track and give their minds a rest by doing something different. When Nick Mimken, the bored head of an insurance agency, took stock of his life and finally realized he wasn't inspired by his work, he decided to sell his business, keep only a few clients, and take sculpture classes. He then went to work as a day laborer for a landscaper in order to pursue his interest in outdoor sculpture—in particular, stone fountains. Today he and his wife live in Nantucket, Massachusetts, where he no longer works *for* a living but *at* living. He is exploring what speaks to him—be it rock sculpture, bronze casting, protecting wildlife, or teaching people how to handle their money. Nick is deeply passionate about his work and how he is living his life. He calls himself a life explorer.

In any event, whether it's an intense, soul-searching exercise or simply a break from corporate life, people almost invariably find time-outs energizing. But stepping out isn't easy. No to-do list, no meetings or phone calls, no structure—it can be difficult for high achievers to abandon their routines. The loss of financial security makes this move inconceivable for some. And for the many people whose identities are tied up in their professional lives, walking away feels like too great a sacrifice. Indeed, we've seen people jump back onto the train within a week or two without reaping any benefit from the time off, just because they could not stand to be away from work.

Find a Program

While a time-out can be little more than a refreshing pause, a leadership or executive development program is a more structured strategy, guiding people as they explore their dreams and open new doors.

Remember John Lauer? Two years after Lauer left BFGoodrich, he was still working with Hungarian refugees (his time-out) and maintained that he wanted nothing to do with running a company. Yet as part of his search for the next phase of his career, he decided to pursue an executive doctorate degree. While in the program, he took a leadership development seminar in which a series of exercises forced him to clarify his values, philosophy, aspirations, and strengths. (See the sidebar "Tools for Reflection" to learn more about some of these exercises.)

In considering the next decade of his life and reflecting on his capabilities, Lauer realized that his resistance to running a company actually represented a fear of replicating his experience at BFGoodrich. In fact, he loved being at the helm of an organization where he could convey his vision and lead the company forward, and he relished working with a team of like-minded executives. Suddenly, he realized that he missed those aspects of the CEO job and that in

Tools for Reflection

ONCE YOU'VE LOST TOUCH WITH YOUR PASSION and dreams, the very routine of work and the habits of your mind can make it difficult to reconnect. Here are some tools that can help people break from those routines and allow their dreams to come to the surface again.

Reflecting on the Past

Alone and with trusted friends and advisers, periodically do a reality check. Take an hour or two and draw your "lifeline." Beginning with childhood, plot the high points and the low points—the events that caused you great joy and great sorrow. Note the times you were most proud, most excited, and most strong and clear. Note also the times you felt lost and alone. Point out for yourself the transitions—times when things fundamentally changed for you. Now, look at the whole. What are some of the underlying themes? What seems to be ever present, no matter the situation? What values seem to weigh in most often and most heavily when you make changes in your life? Are you generally on a positive track, or have there been lots of ups and downs? Where does luck or fate fit in?

Now, switch to the more recent past and consider these questions: What has or has not changed at work, in life? How am I feeling? How do I see myself these days? Am I living my values? Am I having fun? Do my values still fit with what I need to do at work and with what my company is doing? Have my dreams changed? Do I still believe in my vision of my future?

As a way to pull it all together, do a bit of free-form writing, finishing the sentence, "In my life I . . . and now I. . . ."

Defining Your Principles for Life

Think about the different aspects of your life that are important, such as family, relationships, work, spirituality, and physical health. What are your core values in each of those areas? List five or six principles that guide you in life and think about whether they are values that you truly live by or simply talk about.

---

the right kind of situation—one in which he could apply the ideas he'd developed in his studies—being a CEO could be fun.

With this renewed passion to lead, Lauer returned a few headhunters' calls and within a month was offered the job of chairman and CEO at Oglebay Norton, a $250 million company in the

Extending the Horizon

Try writing a page or two about what you would like to do with the rest of your life. Or you might want to number a sheet of paper 1 through 27 and then list all the things you want to do or experience before you die. Don't feel the need to stop at 27, and don't worry about priorities or practicality—just write down whatever comes to you.

This exercise is harder than it seems because it's human nature to think more in terms of what we have to do—by tomorrow, next week, or next month. But with such a short horizon, we can focus only on what's urgent, not on what's important. When we think in terms of the extended horizon, such as what we might do before we die, we open up a new range of possibilities. In our work with leaders who perform this exercise, we've seen a surprising trend: Most people jot down a few career goals, but 80% or more of their lists have nothing to do with work. When they finish the exercise and study their writing, they see patterns that help them begin to crystallize their dreams and aspirations.

Envisioning the Future

Think about where you would be sitting and reading this article if it were 15 years from now and you were living your ideal life. What kinds of people would be around you? How would your environment look and feel? What might you be doing during a typical day or week? Don't worry about the feasibility of creating this life; rather, let the image develop and place yourself in the picture.

Try doing some free-form writing about this vision of yourself, speak your vision into a tape recorder, or talk about it with a trusted friend. Many people report that, when doing this exercise, they experience a release of energy and feel more optimistic than they had even moments earlier. Envisioning an ideal future can be a powerful way to connect with the possibilities for change in our lives.

---

raw-materials business. There he became an exemplar of the democratic leadership style, welcoming employees' input and encouraging his leadership team to do the same. As one of his executives told us, "John raises our spirits, our confidence, and our passion for excellence." Although the company deals in such unglamorous commodities as gravel and sand, Lauer made so many improvements in his first year that Oglebay Norton was featured in *Fortune, BusinessWeek,* and the *Wall Street Journal.*

Another executive we know, Tim Schramko, had a long career managing health care companies. As a diversion, he began teaching part-time. He took on a growing course load while fulfilling his business responsibilities, but he was running himself ragged. It wasn't until he went through a structured process to help him design his ideal future that he realized he had a calling to teach. Once that was clear, he developed a plan for extricating himself from his business obligations over a two-year period and is now a full-time faculty member.

Many educational institutions offer programs that support this type of move. What's more, some companies have developed their own programs in the realization that leaders who have a chance to reconnect with their dreams tend to return with redoubled energy and commitment. The risk, of course, is that after serious reflection, participants will jump ship. But in our experience, most find new meaning and passion in their current positions. In any event, people who do leave weren't in the right job—and they would have realized it sooner or later.

Create "reflective structures"

When leadership guru Warren Bennis interviewed leaders from all walks of life in the early 1990s, he found that they had a common way of staying in touch with what was important to them. They built into their lives what Bennis calls "reflective structures," time and space for self-examination, whether a few hours a week, a day or two a month, or a longer period every year.

For many people, religious practices provide an outlet for reflection, and some people build time into the day or week for prayer or meditation. But reflection does not have to involve organized religion. Exercise is an outlet for many people, and some executives set aside time in their calendars for regular workouts. One CEO of a $2 billion utility company reserves eight hours a week for solitary reflection—an hour a day, perhaps two or three hours on a weekend.

During that time, he might go for a long walk, work in his home shop, or take a ride on his Harley. However you spend the time, the idea is to get away from the demands of your job and be with your own thoughts.

Increasingly, we've seen people seek opportunities for collective reflection as well, so that they can share their dreams and frustrations with their peers. On his third time heading a major division of the Hay Group, Murray Dalziel decided to build some reflection into his life by joining a CEO group that meets once a month. In a sense, the group legitimizes time spent thinking, talking, and learning from one another. Members have created a trusting community where they can share honest feedback—a scarce resource for most executives. And all gain tangible benefits; people exchange tips on how to fix broken processes or navigate sticky situations.

Work with a coach

Our own biases and experiences sometimes make it impossible for us to find a way out of a difficult or confusing situation; we need an outside perspective. Help can come informally from family, friends, and colleagues, or it can come from a professional coach skilled at helping people see their strengths and identify new ways to use them. We won't discuss more traditional therapy in this article, but it is, of course, another alternative.

When Bob McDowell, the HR director, stepped out of his career, he sought out a variety of personal and professional connections to help him decide how to approach the future. Working with an executive coach, McDowell was able to identify what was important to him in life and translate that to what he found essential in a job. He could then draw clear lines around the aspects of his personal life he would no longer compromise, including health and exercise, time with his family, personal hobbies, and other interests. In the end, he found his way to a new career as a partner in an executive search business—a job he'd never considered but one that matched his passion for helping people and the companies they work for. What's more, his soul-searching had so sparked his creativity that in his new position he combined traditional organizational consulting with the search process to discover unusual possibilities. Instead of a typical executive search, he helps companies find employees who will bring magic to the business and to the relationships essential to success.

What did the coach bring to McDowell's self-reflection? Perhaps the chief benefit was a trusting, confidential relationship that gave him the space to dream—something executives shy away from, largely because the expectations of society and their families weigh on them so heavily. Like many, McDowell began this process assuming that he would simply narrow his priorities, clarify his work goals, and chart a new professional path. But to his surprise, his coach's perspective helped him see new opportunities in every part of his life, not just in his work.

Sometimes, however, the coach does little more than help you recognize what you already know at some level. Richard Whiteley, the cofounder of a successful international consulting firm and author of several business bestsellers, felt that he wasn't having as much fun as he used to; he was restless and wanted a change. To that end, he began to do some work on the side, helping business-people improve their effectiveness through spiritual development. He was considering leaving his consulting practice behind altogether and concentrating on the spiritual work—but he was torn. He turned to a spiritual leader, who told him, "Forget the spiritual work and concentrate on the work you've been doing." Only when forced to choose the wrong path could Richard recognize what he truly wanted to do. Within a few months, Richard had devoted himself to writing and speaking almost exclusively on spirituality and passion in work—and he's thriving.

Find new meaning in familiar territory

It's not always feasible to change your job or move somewhere new, even if your situation is undesirable. And frankly, many people don't want to make such major changes. But it is often easier than you might think to make small adjustments so that your work more directly reflects your beliefs and values—as long as you know what you need and have the courage to take some risks.

Back to Niall FitzGerald, who was confronted with the decision over whether to live and work in South Africa. A strong and principled person as well as a good corporate citizen, FitzGerald eventually decided to break with company culture by accepting the job on one unprecedented condition: If over the first six months or so he found his involvement with the country intolerable, he would be allowed to take another job at Unilever, no questions asked. He then set forth to find ways to exert a positive influence on his new work environment wherever possible.

As the leader of a prominent business, FitzGerald had some clout, of course, but he knew that he could not take on the government directly. His response: Figure out what he *could* change, do it, and then deal with the system. For example, when he was building a new plant, the architect showed FitzGerald plans with eight bathrooms—four each for men and women, segregated by the four primary racial groups, as mandated by law. Together, the eight bathrooms would consume one-quarter of an entire floor.

FitzGerald rejected the plans, announcing that he would build two bathrooms, one for men and one for women, to the highest possible standards. Once the plant was built, government officials inspected the building, noticed the discrepancy, and asked him what he planned to do about it. He responded, "They're not segregated because we chose not to do so. We don't agree with segregation. These are very fine toilets . . . you could have your lunch on the floor. . . . I don't have a problem at all. You have a problem, and you have to decide what you are going to do. I'm doing nothing." The government did not respond immediately, but later the law was quietly changed. FitzGerald's act of rebellion was small, but it was consistent with his values and was the only stand he could have taken in good conscience. Living one's values in this way, in the face of opposition, is energizing. Bringing about change that can make a difference to the people around us gives meaning to our work, and for many people, it leads to a renewed commitment to their jobs.

For Rob, the manager who found himself reporting to an abusive boss, the first step was to look inward and admit that every day would be a challenge. By becoming very clear about his own core values, he could decide moment to moment how to deal with Martin's demands. He could determine whether a particular emotional reaction was a visceral response to a man he didn't respect or a reaction to a bad idea that he would need to confront. He could choose whether to do what he thought was right or to collude with what felt wrong. His clarity allowed him to stay calm and focused, do his job well, and take care of the business and the people around him. In the end, Rob came out of a difficult situation knowing he had kept his integrity without compromising his career, and in that time, he even learned and grew professionally. He still uses the barometer he developed during his years with Martin to check actions and decisions against his values, even though his circumstances have changed.

Another executive we've worked with, Bart Morrison, ran a nonprofit organization for ten years and was widely considered a success by donors, program recipients, and policy makers alike. Yet he felt restless and wondered if a turn as a company executive—which would mean higher compensation—would satisfy his urge for a new challenge. Morrison didn't really need more money, although it would have been a plus, and he had a deep sense of social mission and commitment to his work. He also acknowledged that working in the private sector would not realistically offer him any meaningful new challenges. In our work together, he brainstormed about different avenues he could take while continuing in the nonprofit field, and it occurred to him that he could write books and give speeches. These new activities gave him the excitement he had been looking for and allowed him to stay true to his calling.

It's worth noting that executives often feel threatened when employees start asking, "Am I doing what I want to do with my life?" The risk is very real that the answer will be no, and companies can lose great contributors. The impulse, then, may be to try to suppress such exploration. Many executives also avoid listening to their own signals, fearing that a close look at their dreams and aspirations will reveal severe disappointments, that to be true to themselves they will have to leave their jobs and sacrifice everything they have worked so hard to achieve.

But although people no longer expect leaders to have all the answers, they do expect their leaders to be open to the questions—to try to keep their own passion alive and to support employees through the same process. After all, sooner or later most people will feel an urgent need to take stock—and if they are given the chance to heed the call, they will most likely emerge stronger, wiser, and more determined than ever.

Originally published in April 2002. Reprint R0204G

Next-Gen Retirement

by Heather C. Vough, Christine D. Bataille,
Leisa Sargent, and Mary Dean Lee

EVERY DAY IN THE UNITED STATES more than 10,000 people turn 65. For decades this was the typical retirement age. Starting in their early fifties, but certainly by age 70, people were expected to end their careers and embrace a life of leisure. But in the past 20 years, that paradigm has shifted dramatically. Half of today's 60-year-olds will live to at least age 90, according to Lynda Gratton and Andrew Scott, the authors of *The 100-Year Life,* which draws on the research of demographers Jim Oeppen and James Vaupel. Meanwhile, the era of corporate and government pension plans that promised lifetime financial security is over. For this and other reasons, many executives are now rethinking what it means to retire.

Researchers have spent a great deal of time investigating how organizations should respond to (and take advantage of) this trend. Indeed, a 2004 HBR article coauthored by Ken Dychtwald, an expert on aging, argued that companies should "retire retirement," keeping older workers engaged by creating cultures that value experience and allowing flexible schedules and exit plans.

In our work with executives, we've also become interested in how individuals are approaching 21st-century retirement. To explore the different paths being taken, we partnered with Jelena Zikic of York University to conduct in-depth interviews with 100 executives and managers who had recently retired or were actively considering it. We also interviewed HR professionals from 24 companies in the sectors where most of our study participants worked (financial services, natural resources, and high-tech manufacturing) to get a broader view of retirement today. We focused on managers because their departures have important organizational implications, and these people are more likely to have the financial means to make choices about when and how they retire.

We found much more variation in these individuals' opinions and experiences than traditional theories and clichés had led us to expect. In this article we summarize our findings. From the insights gathered, we've extrapolated four guiding principles that should help people of any generation navigate their late-career journeys: Prepare to go off-script; find your own retirement metaphor; create a new deal; and make a difference.

Prepare to Go Off-Script

In listening to managers tell their stories, we discovered that very few had made a clear-cut, irrevocable shift from full-time work to retirement when they reached a certain age or eligibility. Their careers ended in many ways, often on unpredictable timetables. While some managers did describe "following the [traditional] script," others talked about "identifying a window" of opportunity when retirement felt right; "having an epiphany" because health or other events prompted a reorientation away from work; "cashing out" with a generous package; "becoming disillusioned" by organizational changes; and "being discarded"—essentially pushed out of a job or an organization. In sum, a number of factors influenced the way their retirements played out.

Consider Louis, 56, the general manager of a large division of an international telecommunications firm, who had spent 32 years at his company. He decided to retire earlier than expected when his employer appointed a man he didn't respect to be the new CEO. Although Louis stayed on for two years to help with a reorganization, he left as soon as he felt he could. Alan, 49, a successful and well-respected regional sales manager for a manufacturing company, had a similar story. After his firm changed ownership and was restructured, he was given three options: a lateral move involving

Idea in Brief

With longevity increasing and thousands of Baby Boomers turning 65 every day, the face of retirement is changing. Interviews with executives and managers conducted by the authors show that very few people now follow the tradition of ditching the job and embracing a life of leisure in their midsixties. This article describes the different paths being taken and offers four principles that will help you navigate your late-career journey:

1. **Prepare to go off-script.** Careers end in many ways—often unpredictably. Most of us will have little control over our exit, so we must be ready to adapt.

2. **Find your metaphor.** Do you see retirement as *liberation* from the grind, the *loss* of your professional identity, or a chance for *transformation*? The language that resonates most with you can signal your best way forward.

3. **Create a new deal.** Many are stepping back gradually or staying on at their firms with redesigned schedules and responsibilities or as contractors. Explore the possibilities.

4. **Make a difference.** Shelving your expertise at retirement no longer makes sense. The new model is to apply your talents to improve your community and the world.

geographical relocation, a demotion, or an early retirement package. Although he initially felt he was too young to retire, he decided it would be in his best interest to accept the package.

The lesson here is that few of us will have complete control over when and how our careers end, so we should all get ready to improvise and adapt. Mergers and acquisitions, shifts in management or strategic direction, restructurings, and unexpected personal events may not lead to an immediate exit, but they can set things in motion. No matter how well thought out your plan for retirement may be, there is a good chance things won't turn out exactly as you'd hoped.

Find Your Retirement Metaphor

Managers use a variety of language when talking about retirement. (See the table "What does 'retirement' mean to you?") Some think of it as *detox* from work stress, *liberation* from the daily grind, or

---

What does "retirement" mean to you?

Executives in their fifties and sixties use various metaphors to describe their post-career plans. Here are some of the most common:

Loss	A lack of purpose, a fear of being forgotten, or a threat to your identity
Renaissance	A new beginning, a new chapter, or a "blank canvas" offering possibilities to pursue your interests or passions
Detox	The "cleansing" experience of getting away from an unhealthy, stressful working life
Liberation	Being released from the constraints and restrictions of work; running toward a newfound freedom
Downshifting	Gaining time through the transition to a slower pace of life
Staying the course	Continued engagement and contribution; using your professional skills in different settings
Milestone	Reaching a pinnacle and achieving a goal; a marker of the end of one phase and the beginning of another
Transformation	A positive adaptation to a new role or lifestyle; taking on a new identity

Note: This table has been adapted from one the authors published in the *Journal of Vocational Behavior* in October 2011.

---

downshifting from a demanding career. Those metaphors all aptly describe the experiences of Jim, who retired from his position as the CEO of an international company when he was barely 50 because of a health scare. His father had died in his forties, and Jim didn't want to follow in his footsteps. Others envision a *renaissance* in their lives or a chance at *transformation*. Take Margaret, who stepped down from a demanding job in marketing and strategic planning at a consumer goods company to become an executive-in-residence at a prestigious business school. Still others regard retirement as a *milestone* in their career, worry about the *loss* of professional identity, or imagine *staying the course* and continuing to put their skills to use. A good example of the last is Bill, a geologist, who retired quite early from the oil company that had employed him for 25 years but soon decided to resume work by starting an oil-drilling venture with a colleague.

As people grow into retirement, however, their perspective on it often evolves. Some who initially see it as, say, liberation—the freedom to pursue golf or bridge or take cruises—can move into staying-the-course, transformation, or renaissance modes. Consider the rest of Jim's story. His first years of retirement were about unwinding and recovering from an all-consuming job, but he also began to miss aspects of his high-flying career. He first turned his attention to his family but eventually resumed a professional life coaching ambitious young managers.

In our research we found that individuals who take a flexible approach and are willing to shift from one metaphor to another are able to craft a retirement that feels right for them. So, especially if you're approaching this major life transition, take a moment to reflect on what it means to you. What images pop into your mind? Which, if any, of the metaphors we've described match your dreams and desires? If none of them resonate, is there another path for you? The idea is to better understand yourself, your perspectives on your work and your life, who you want to be going forward, and all the new activities or identities open to you.

Remember, too, that you can travel multiple paths in retirement. That versatility will be even more important for future generations. According to Gratton and Scott, people who are 20 years old today have a 50% chance of living to 100, while those who are 40 have the same odds of reaching 95. Even if you end your career at 75, you will probably want to try more than one type of retirement.

Create a New Deal

Rather than completely retiring, many professionals are striking deals to stay on at their organizations with redesigned schedules or responsibilities. Take Daniel, a senior executive at a financial institution who negotiated to continue his employment on a half-time basis. Now, for two weeks a month, he retreats to a fishing-and-hunting cabin in the coastal wilderness. But for the other two weeks,

Daniel returns to corporate headquarters as a "thought leader" and mentor to up-and-coming executives. Another seasoned manager who participated in our study proposed a three-way job share with two colleagues who had young children. He wanted to step back but stay engaged; his coworkers wanted to keep developing their careers on family-friendly schedules; and their high-tech firm agreed to the plan.

Often executives take a phased retirement approach—gradually reducing their hours while helping to transfer knowledge and responsibility to their successors. For example, after reaching his pensionable retirement age, Mark, a senior forestry executive, negotiated to work on a 60% basis. That way, he could keep contributing to his company—in particular, by mentoring two teams of managers and helping with succession planning—but also respond to some pressing health issues. Over time he cut back his hours.

Another alternative is to arrange contract work with a former employer. Such deals benefit both the individuals (who receive compensation and the opportunity to reengage) and the organization (which can recapture lost expertise). Six months after Peter, a banker in his midfifties, retired, his former employer asked him to return on a contract basis to fill a role requiring his unique small-business-loan expertise.

Yet another exit path was taken by Adam, who in his early fifties requested a two-year leave of absence to serve as a city councillor. He returned to his firm for a time and then at age 56 formally retired from it, going on to lead a large community organization.

We encourage anyone considering retirement to explore different ways of staying or leaving. Take a hard look at what you do, at your unique experience, skills, and knowledge, and at how your employer views you. Reflect on the various roles you've had, projects you've completed, and where you've made the most meaningful contributions and felt most satisfied.

Not all organizations can facilitate innovative, one-off work roles or arrangements, but there may be more room to maneuver than you think. Once you have a good sense of the contribution you would like to make and your preferred schedule, broach the idea informally with your superiors or human resource managers. If they're unwilling to explore flexible options for staying on or transitioning out or to provide what you're looking for, consider reaching out to other organizations, which may be delighted to offer that flexibility.

Make a Difference

Retirement has long been seen as a time when people turn to philanthropic pursuits, perhaps following Andrew Carnegie's advice to spend the first third of your life getting educated, the second third getting rich, and the last third giving the money away. But we found that many of today's retirees are making much more than financial contributions to society. A few examples: After unexpectedly being fired in his early sixties, Harry, an engineer-turned-plant-manager in the pulp-and-paper industry, started working with high school dropouts to help them acquire marketable skills. Linda, a management training and development expert with 28 years of experience at a bank, retired at 50 and then went back to college to study international development with the intention of founding an orphanage for African children who'd lost their parents to AIDS. Sylvia, a successful investment banker close to burnout, retired early and took a big (unpaid) job as treasurer on the board of a major cultural institution. Gary, a telecommunications executive, left his position to launch a new venture to fund start-ups with social missions.

When you expect to live much longer, in better mental and physical health, the idea of shelving your expertise in retirement no longer makes sense. The new precedent—one that will no doubt be embraced by future generations, especially the socially conscious Millennials—is for retirees to leverage their knowledge, skill, and talent to make a difference in their communities or the world. Even if you're tired of the specific work you've been doing, your leadership, teamwork, and project management know-how can be applied to a host of other activities. Retirement is not an end but a beginning—an opportunity to experiment and explore, to engage in pursuits you value, and perhaps to reinvent your legacy.

Originally published in June 2016. Reprint R1606J

About the Contributors

ROBIN ABRAHAMS is a research associate at Harvard Business School.

ERIKA ANDERSEN is the founding partner of Proteus International and the author of *Growing Great Employees, Being Strategic, Leading So People Will Follow,* and the forthcoming *Be Bad First.*

RON ASHKENAS is a coauthor of the *Harvard Business Review Leader's Handbook* and a Partner Emeritus at Schaffer Consulting. His previous books include *The Boundaryless Organization, The GE Work-Out,* and *Simply Effective.*

KEN BANTA is the founder and principal of the Vanguard Group for Leadership.

CHRISTINE D. BATAILLE is an assistant professor at the Ithaca College School of Business.

ORLAN BOSTON is a partner in the Ernst & Young LLP Global Health Sciences practice.

RICHARD BOYATZIS is a Professor in the Departments of Organizational Behavior, Psychology, and Cognitive Science at the Weatherhead School of Management and Distinguished University Professor at Case Western Reserve University. He is a cofounder of the Coaching Research Lab and coauthor of *Helping People Change* (Harvard Business Review Press, 2019).

BRIANNA BARKER CAZA is an Associate Professor of Management in the Bryan School of Business and Economics at the University of North Carolina at Greensboro.

PETER F. DRUCKER was a professor of social science and management at Claremont Graduate University in California.

JANE DUTTON is the Robert L. Kahn Distinguished University Professor of Business Administration and Psychology at the University of Michigan's Ross School of Business. She is cofounder of the Center for Positive Organizations at Ross.

DANIEL GOLEMAN, a codirector of the Consortium for Research on Emotional Intelligence in Organizations at Rutgers University, is the author of *Focus: The Hidden Driver of Excellence* (HarperCollins, 2013) and other books, including *Building Blocks of Emotional Intelligence*.

BORIS GROYSBERG is the Richard P. Chapman Professor of Business Administration at Harvard Business School, Faculty Affiliate at the HBS Gender Initiative, and the coauthor, with Michael Slind, of *Talk, Inc.* (Harvard Business Review Press, 2012).

EMILY HEAPHY is an Assistant Professor of Management at the Isenberg School of Management at the University of Massachusetts Amherst.

MARK LEE HUNTER is an adjunct professor at INSEAD.

HERMINIA IBARRA is the Charles Handy Professor of Organizational Behavior at London Business School. Prior to joining LBS, she served on the INSEAD and Harvard Business School faculties. She is the author of *Act Like a Leader, Think Like a Leader* (Harvard Business Review Press, 2015).

MARY DEAN LEE is a professor emeritus in the Desautels Faculty of Management, McGill University.

JOSHUA D. MARGOLIS is the James Dinan and Elizabeth Miller Professor of Business Administration and the head of the Organizational Behavior unit at Harvard Business School.

MITCHELL LEE MARKS is a leadership professor at San Francisco State University's College of Business and the president of JoiningForces. org.

ANNIE McKEE is a senior fellow at the University of Pennsylvania Graduate School of Education and the director of the PennCLO Executive Doctoral Program. She is the author of *How to Be Happy at Work* and a coauthor of *Primal Leadership*, *Resonant Leadership*, and *Becoming a Resonant Leader*.

PHILIP MIRVIS is an organizational psychologist and consultant who has authored twelve books including *Beyond Good Company: Next Generation Corporate Citizenship*.

ROBERT QUINN is a professor emeritus at the University of Michigan's Ross School of Business and a cofounder of the school's Center for Positive Organizations.

LAURA MORGAN ROBERTS is a professor of practice at the University of Virginia's Darden School of Business, and the co-editor of *Race, Work, and Leadership: New Perspectives on the Black Experience* (Harvard Business Review Press, 2019).

LEISA SARGENT is a professor at UNSW Australia Business School.

GRETCHEN SPREITZER is the Keith E. and Valerie J. Alessi Professor of Business Administration at the University of Michigan's Ross School of Business, where she is a core faculty member in the Center for Positive Organizations.

PAUL G. STOLTZ is CEO of PEAK Learning, Inc., founder and managing director of the GRII Institute and the Global Resilience Institute, and the originator of the Adversity Quotient (AQ) theory and method, currently used within Harvard Business School's Executive Education program.

HEATHER C. VOUGH is an assistant professor at the University of Cincinnati's Lindner College of Business.

Index

The most important management ideas all in one place.

We hope you enjoyed this book from *Harvard Business Review*. Now you can get even more with HBR's 10 Must Reads Boxed Set. From books on leadership and strategy to managing yourself and others, this 6-book collection delivers articles on the most essential business topics to help you succeed.

HBR's 10 Must Reads Series

The definitive collection of ideas and best practices on our most sought-after topics from the best minds in business.

- Change Management
- Collaboration
- Communication
- Emotional Intelligence
- Innovation
- Leadership
- Making Smart Decisions

- Managing Across Cultures
- Managing People
- Managing Yourself
- Strategic Marketing
- Strategy
- Teams
- The Essentials

hbr.org/mustreads

Buy for your team, clients, or event.
Visit hbr.org/bulksales for quantity discount rates.